P9-DDP-463

Living with the World

SEPTEMBER 12, 1964.

A New Treasury of Words to Live By

Selected and Interpreted by
Ninety Eminent Men and Women
Edited by

William Nichols

SIMON AND SCHUSTER

ALL RIGHTS RESERVED
INCLUDING THE RIGHT OF REPRODUCTION
IN WHOLE OR IN PART IN ANY FORM
COPYRIGHT © 1947, 1948, 1949, 1950, 1951, 1952, 1953, 1954, 1955, 1956, 1957, 1958, 1959, BY UNITED NEWSPAPERS MAGAZINE CORPORATION
PUBLISHED BY SIMON AND SCHUSTER, INC.
ROCKEFELLER CENTER, 630 FIFTH AVENUE
NEW YORK 20, N. Y.

ACKNOWLEDGMENTS

Permission has been granted to reprint the following material:

From *The Art of Loving,* copyright © 1956 by Erich Fromm. By permission of Harper & Brothers.

From *Education and Freedom* by Vice Admiral H. G. Rickover. Copyright © 1958 by H. G. Rickover. Reprinted by permission of E. P. Dutton & Co., Inc.

The lines by Boris Pasternak, from an interview by Nils Ake Nilsson in *The Reporter,* November 27, 1958. Reprinted by permission of *The Reporter* and of Kurt Bernheim.

LIBRARY OF CONGRESS CATALOG CARD NUMBER: 59-9494
MANUFACTURED IN THE UNITED STATES OF AMERICA

"No one saves us but ourselves;
No one can and no one may,
We ourselves must walk the Path,
Teachers merely show the way."

—NANCY WILSON ROSS,
"The Return of Lady Brace"

Contents

PART TWO: LIVING WITH OTHER PEOPLE

PART THREE: LIVING WITH THE WORLD

PART FOUR: "IT GOES ON!"

Introduction

THE "WORDS TO LIVE BY" series in *This Week* magazine was born in 1947, at a time when Americans were seeking to adjust from wartime conditions back to the uneasy terms of atomic peace.

The idea for the series stemmed from the reading of a book by David Grayson which told stories about rural life in his New England village. One character appealed to me immediately. He was a farmer, and whenever he ran across some bit of verse or prose he liked he slipped the words inside his hatband, to be tacked up later on his granary wall.

"I thought afterward," Grayson wrote, "how most of us have collections of sayings we live by. . . . I believe it would be difficult to find an adult human being who hasn't a saying or two, or more, that he is saving because it expresses something vital."

"Words to Live By" was conceived not as essays that would teach people, or preach at them, but as a collection of such "sayings" combined with the actual experience of the people who chose them. It was to provide, in terms of contemporary America—and for the thirteen million families who receive *This Week*—the modern equivalent of David Grayson's granary wall.

Because the quotations had caught fire in minds accustomed to important enterprises of thought, I hoped they would express "something vital" to millions of others. From this sharing process we could all benefit, at a time when so many people are seeking to rediscover and reaffirm the basic values of life.

That our hopes were justified is attested by many reactions. One of the most gratifying was this comment from Kenneth Roberts, written shortly after publication of the first collection of *Words to Live By:*

"I had no expectations whatever, yet here I find a book loaded with character revelations that are unique. The rubbing together of minds has produced a fountain of ideas."

Equally rewarding were the many letters from readers, indicating the almost magic power of the "sharing" process. Typical is the following from a reader in St. Clair Shores, Michigan:

"For some time now I have wanted to write and thank you for 'Words to Live By.' It is truly that. Each week it seems to have a message just for me. Yet as I talk to others, they also feel the same."

Contributors to the series have also experienced the same direct and intimate response. Cameron Hawley, for example, wrote me as follows after publication of his little article, which appears on page 189 in this volume:

"I have been simply bowled over by the amount of reaction there has been to my little 'Words to Live By' piece. Letters have been coming from all over the country. As you know, I have written for almost every magazine in the country but I don't think I have ever done a piece that brought more reaction from readers."

More than a dozen years have passed since the appearance of the first contribution to "Words to Live By." In that time, upwards of six hundred men and women have shared their thoughts with the readers of *This Week* magazine. In 1948, the present publishers asked me to collect some of the more significant pieces in a book. The anthology was revised the following year, but there has been no revision since.

This is an entirely new collection, with one or two exceptions noted in the text, of the pieces which have appeared on the "Words to Live By" page since 1950. They are grouped into sections which follow the four human relationships—man with himself, with other people, with the larger world and, finally, with God and the infinite. These groups are followed by two sections of more homely philosophy—"When I Was a Child" and "Ways of Life"—which contain some of the truths handed down within families, rules that shape the mold of American character. In a final section, the reader is once again encouraged to join in the sharing and record his own Words to Live By.

The continued need for such sharing was proclaimed dramatically in 1958, when the important Rockefeller Report on

Education was published. In it are these significant words: *"What most people want—young or old—is not merely security, or comfort, or luxury, although they are glad enough to have these. Most of all, they want meaning in their lives. If our era and our culture and our leaders do not, or cannot, offer great meanings, great objectives, great convictions, then people will settle for shallow and trivial substitutes. This is a deficicency for which we all bear a responsibility. . . . This is the challenge of our times."*

In effect, the "Words to Live By" series, on which this book is based, represents an effort to meet this challenge in terms of our times and of the many million families who receive *This Week* magazine each Sunday.

It has been an invigorating experience to work with people and to see them through the words they live by. It has been inspiring to learn from thousands of reader letters how far-spread is the appreciation of the wisdom and challenge these brief pieces contain. The sum of such letters is heartening affirmation that Americans everywhere are ready to respond to "great meanings, great objectives and great convictions." And I am grateful to the many contributors in this series, who have helped to provide them.

WILLIAM NICHOLS

New York City
January 25, 1959

PART ONE

Living With Yourself

1

Setting the Goal

Start Living!

BY

CORNELIA OTIS SKINNER

WRITER, ACTRESS AND MONOLOGIST

"We are always getting ready to live, but never living."

—RALPH WALDO EMERSON

MY FATHER, Otis Skinner, was a highly successful director as well as an actor. When directing, he had one bit of advice to pass on to the nervous player. "Take the pins out of your diaphragm, my friend," he would say, "and start breathing!" This always had the instant effect of loosening the jittery actor's tension of voice and body and easing him into a freer and better performance.

Father once gave me similar advice, if under dissimilar circumstances. I was twenty-three and going through a trying period of introspection and immature gloom. My attitude of "Oh, the pain of it all!" was an acute pain in the neck to my family. Father put up with me for a time. Then one day while we were taking a long walk in the country, he shook me out of my Byronic miasma with an amused but understanding "Take the pins out of your diaphragm, kid, and start living!"

I can't say that I started living just then, but his words gave me a sudden new perspective of myself. A sorry sight it was: a youthful egotist so tensed up in self-absorption she had ceased to breathe deeply of the life around her.

Even today the advice holds good for me. God knows, these are days of tension for everyone. But we are all too prone to fight tension with further tensions, senseless distractions, incessant entertainment, the obsession of keeping busy —often with activities of little value. Or we resort to an ostrich head-in-the-sand negation with liquor, easy love affairs and the latest brand of tranquilizer—anything to avoid an ever deepening awareness of being alive.

Life isn't easy, but in the long run it's easier than going to elaborate ends to deny it. We might do worse than "take the pins out of our diaphragms and start living."

Finding Yourself

BY

CHARLES JACKSON

AUTHOR OF "THE LOST WEEKEND,"
"EARTHLY CREATURES"

"O wad some Pow'r the giftie gie us To see oursels as ithers see us!"

—ROBERT BURNS

OUR TEEN-AGED DAUGHTER came home the other day with one of those amazed if commonplace discoveries peculiar to the young. After school she had gone with some pals to an ice-cream joint, the back room of which was lined with mirrors. "It was the darnedest thing!" she said. "I saw this girl's profile in the glass and I stared and stared, wondering who she was, when all of a sudden I realized it was me. All the time it was me!" she cried, carried away by her astonishment to the point of throwing to the winds her usually impeccable grammar. "Why, she looked no more like me than, why, than anything! I didn't know I looked like that!"

We've all had a similar experience at one time or another; and I could have told her further—and further raised her eyebrows—that if by some magic she could watch herself walking along the street, she would not recognize or even know who it was; but if it were one of her friends, she could spot the identity and name the girl after no more than the most casual glance.

Why this should be true is one of those baffling mysteries; but true it is, all the same. Not for nothing did Bobbie Burns write his famous couplet, concluding cogently that such a gift would "frae monie a blunder free us, An' foolish notion." Twenty centuries before that Plato said it even more simply with his two words *"Know thyself."*

Offhand—and that is the deadly, the delusive part of it—it would seem as easy as pie to know oneself. After all, whom do we spend more time with? With whose most intimate thoughts are we in more constant exchange? But it isn't as easy as that; and the older we grow, the more we realize it. Our real identity, our innermost self, eludes us, leaving us with the frustrated but resigned certainty that if we really knew who we were, the complex business of life would be simpler.

Repeatedly the baffling question comes up: Why did I do

this, or that, today? Why did I lose my temper? Or take that extra drink? Or say hurtful things to someone whose love I sorely want? Why—and why—and why?

Nor do mirrors give us any help. We gaze searchingly into the glass, and all we see there is the reflection of the face we present to the world. The realer self lies somewhere within, unknown but only too evidently there (for we cannot fool ourselves). It may well be that ultimate self-knowledge will come only with the final moment. Meanwhile we try harder, more honestly, as the years pass.

Sometimes we find a clue in some chance remark by an old friend, a bit read in some wise book, a fleeting thought during a moment of deep feeling and deeper meditation. Thus, bit by bit, self-knowledge grows. But it does not come easy and perhaps this very awareness of the difficulty sustains us, spurs us on toward the ever receding goal. For the self-knowledge we seek—rising above our social vanities, and pride, and the impression we wish to make on friends—is a full-time, lifetime job.

Liking Yourself

BY

JOHN STEINBECK

AUTHOR

"That which we are, we are . . ."
—ALFRED, LORD TENNYSON

ONCE A FRIEND of mine named Ed said to me, "For a very long time I didn't like myself." It was not said in self-pity but simply as an unfortunate fact. "It was a very difficult time," he said, "and very painful. I did not like myself for a number of reasons, some of them valid and some of them pure fancy. I would hate to have to go back to that.

"Then gradually," he said, "I discovered with surprise and pleasure that a number of people did like me. And I thought, If they can like me, why can't I like myself? Just thinking it did not do it, but slowly I learned to like myself and then it was all right."

This was not said in self-love in its bad connotation but in self-knowledge. He meant literally that he had learned to accept and like the person Ed as he liked other people. It gave him a great advantage. Most people do not like themselves at all. They distrust themselves, put on masks and pomposities. They quarrel and boast and pretend and are jealous because they do not like themselves. But mostly they do not even know themselves well enough to form a true liking, and since we automatically fear and dislike strangers, we fear and dislike our stranger-selves.

Once Ed was able to like himself he was released from the secret prison of self-contempt.

I wish we could all be so. If we could learn to like ourselves even a little, maybe our cruelties and angers might melt away. Maybe we would not have to hurt one another just to keep our ego chins above water.

Do You Want to Be Wise? Rich? Famous?

BY

DOROTHY VAN DOREN

EDITOR AND AUTHOR

"God says: Take what you want and pay for it!"
—SPANISH PROVERB

WHEN I FIRST heard this stern proverb from Spain it frightened me; I used to dream of an Angel with a flaming sword. But as I thought more about it, I realized that the Angel held not a sword but a balance.

In one side you put what you would like to be. Do you want to be famous? Very well, says the Angel, then spend every waking hour in the pursuit of fame. It will show up on the other side of the balance in time spent and sacrifices made. Is it riches you want? Think about money every day, study it, give your life to it, and the balance will be weighted with gold—but at the cost of other things.

Maybe you want to be wise. The Angel will weigh out a high payment for that, too; it will include a good life, a pursuit of knowledge, and an uncompromising love of truth.

Everything has its price. We are familiar with this idea in our daily lives. We go to the self-service store. In our wire cart we put a can of tomatoes, a bit of cheese, bread, hamburger and spaghetti. On the way out the clerk adds up our bill, puts our purchases in a paper bag, and we carry home our dinner—after we have paid for it.

So with the balance of our lives: on one side, our heart's desire; on the other side of the scales, the reckoning. When the scales are even, you may take out what you have bought. Sometimes the price seems high. But remember, you must pay for the character and quality of your goal as well as for the achievement of it. The law is simple and it is just; you may have what you want—but you must pay. *Nothing is free.*

You *Are* What You *Do*

BY

MADAME CHIANG KAI-SHEK

". . . whatsoever a man soweth, that shall he also reap."

—GALATIANS, 6:7

IF THE PAST has taught us anything it is that every cause brings its effect, every action has a consequence. This thought, in my opinion, is the moral foundation of the universe; it applies equally in this world and the next.

We Chinese have a saying: "If a man plants melons he will reap melons; if he sows beans, he will reap beans." And this is true of every man's life; good begets good, and evil leads to evil.

True enough, the sun shines on the saint and the sinner alike, and too often it seems that the wicked wax and prosper. But we can say with certitude that, with the individual as with the nation, the flourishing of the wicked is an illusion, for, unceasingly, life keeps books on us all.

In the end, we are all the sum total of our actions. Character cannot be counterfeited, nor can it be put on and cast off as if it were a garment to meet the whim of the moment. Like the markings on wood which are ingrained in the very heart of the tree, character requires time and nurture for growth and development.

Thus also, day by day, we write our own destiny; for inexorably we become what we do. This, I believe, is the supreme logic and the law of life.

The Uncommon Man

BY

HERBERT HOOVER

FORMER PRESIDENT OF THE UNITED STATES

"That nation is proudest and noblest and most exalted which has the greatest number of really great men."

—SINCLAIR LEWIS

IN MY OPINION, we are in danger of developing a cult of the Common Man, which means a cult of mediocrity. But there is at least one hopeful sign: I have never been able to find out just who this Common Man is. In fact, most Americans—especially women—will get mad and fight if you try calling them common.

This is hopeful because it shows that most people are holding fast to an essential fact in American life. We believe in equal opportunity for all, but we know that this includes the opportunity to rise to leadership. In other words—to be uncommon!

Let us remember that the great human advances have not been brought about by mediocre men and women. They were brought about by distinctly uncommon people with vital sparks of leadership. Many great leaders were of humble origin, but that alone was not their greatness.

It is a curious fact that when you get sick you want an uncommon doctor; if your car breaks down you want an uncommonly good mechanic; when we get into war we want dreadfully an uncommon admiral and an uncommon general.

I have never met a father and mother who did not want their children to grow up to be uncommon men and women. May it always be so. For the future of America rests not in mediocrity, but in the constant renewal of leadership in every phase of our national life.

EDITOR'S NOTE: *The article above first appeared on the "Words to Live By" page in* THIS WEEK *on February 6, 1949, and has since been widely reprinted. We reprint it now again, as an eloquent reminder of America's greatest need: the pursuit of excellence.*

The Larger Aim

BY

NATHAN M. PUSEY

PRESIDENT OF HARVARD UNIVERSITY

"It is essential that we enable young people to see themselves as participants in one of the most exciting eras in history, and to have a sense of purpose in relation to it."

—ROCKEFELLER REPORT ON EDUCATION

NOT LONG AGO I was disturbed to read a newspaper report of a student's speech which maintained that today's college senior views his education simply as a means toward "a better-paying job . . . more security . . . social position."

If there are students who seriously believe this, then it seems to me they have missed the main point of college—or indeed of being alive—and that we are in for trouble.

The true liberal education has larger aims than just cramming its students with facts in order to teach them how to earn a living. First, it must help each student to find himself as an individual; then it must help him to lose himself in interests, causes, and ideas larger and more enduring than he is.

America has no need for a race of young people fitted to the same pattern, content to sit back and enjoy what has been called "a prosperous conformity." But our country will always have room for imaginative, reasonable, and responsible men and women. And it desperately needs the informed and the truly creative among its young people.

I believe the teacher's mission is to help every young person in his care grow into the broadest, deepest, most vital person possible. And in fulfilling himself the student will, I am convinced, arrive at moments of heightened insight when he sees more clearly than ever before what the world is about and how he can fit into it creatively and significantly.

Viewed this way, a college education suddenly takes on new meaning—and so do the staggering estimates of college enrollment. Instead of a frightening prospect of millions of young people solely concerned with a scramble for better jobs, we can look forward confidently to a challenging tomorrow when millions of young Americans turn to college because they want to realize their full capacity as human beings, to find major pleasure in learning, to live richly and responsibly, and to do their part to help create a better world.

How I Found Peace

BY

H. V. KALTENBORN

VETERAN NEWS ANALYST

"This above all: to thine own self be true,
And it must follow, as the night the day,
Thou canst not then be false to any man."
—WILLIAM SHAKESPEARE

FOR MORE THAN fifty years as reporter, editor and radio commentator, I have tried to live up to this bit of good counsel with which Polonius sent Laertes on his way.

Every man sets himself a certain standard; the hard thing is to live up to it. In my line of work, that of analyzing and interpreting the news of the day for millions of readers and listeners, the temptation to serve something other than the public interest is constant. The human instinct to protect friends, the natural desire to escape criticism, the direct or indirect pressure from business and editorial associates, the more or less legitimate demands of an advertising sponsor are always raising ethical issues.

Without some guiding principle it is not easy to know what to do. The simplest way out is to yield to pressure. But that undermines character and makes it more difficult to resist the next demand.

As a boy I studied the lives of our great American editors and learned that they became great because they had the courage and independence to be true to themselves. That became my ambition: to make the public cause my cause and to serve it regardless of cost or consequence. I have not always been right, alas, but I have been true to myself even when I was wrong. And, for half a century, I have had peace of mind.

The Greatest Art

BY

MYLES CONNOLLY

AUTHOR OF "THE BUMP ON BRANNIGAN'S HEAD"

"It is something to be able to paint a particular picture, or to carve a statue, and so to make a few objects beautiful; but it is far more glorious to carve and paint the very atmosphere and medium through which we look . . . To affect the quality of the day—that is the highest of arts."

—HENRY THOREAU

IN THESE WORDS, Thoreau is trying to remind us that great art is not restricted exclusively to such pursuits as painting, music, sculpture and writing. There is an art of living, too.

One can find an artist's work inspiring, while at the same time his life is common, petty, even sordid.

In contrast, Thoreau makes us think of such people as St.

Francis of Assisi, Gandhi, Florence Nightingale—not artists in the usual sense but persons who, through the nobility of their lives, affected the "quality of the day." There is no limit to the number of such artists. It includes the countless obscure, good people who quietly affect the lives of those about them without even being aware they are doing it, winning no commendation, expecting none.

Everybody must at one time or another have known such persons, strangers as well as relatives or friends, who have changed the quality of the day for him. They come into a room in a dark hour—a sickroom, say, or a death room, a room without hope, or merely in an hour when we are lonely or discouraged. They may say little, if anything. But the shining quality of goodness radiates from them, from their mere presence, and where there was dark there is light, or the beginning of light; where there was cowardice there is courage; where there was listlessness there is love of life.

These friends and relatives—or wonderful strangers met at a picnic, in a lifeboat, a hospital waiting room—all these, humble and unaware, carry with them the kindness and generosity of their lives. These, it seems to me, are the greatest artists. For they practice the highest of the arts—the art of life itself.

2

The Happy Road

Where Happiness Begins

BY

DONALD CULROSS PEATTIE

AUTHOR AND NATURALIST

"There is no duty we underrate so much as the duty of being happy."

—ROBERT LOUIS STEVENSON

NOW THERE'S A BIT of morality as manly as it is smiling! I never did become convinced of what I was so smugly told in childhood: "Be good and you will be happy." Whereas I am quite sure that if you are happy you will be good.

People who generate this inner sunshine make life pleasanter for those around them. Their impulses lead to right action; their thoughts are usually true. They have their roots in some deep, shining faith.

Now, anyone can be in good spirits when the luck is running his way. But happiness is not always the result of fortune. It is frequently a virtue, and a brave one. Happiness comes of the grace to accept life gratefully and make the most of the best of it.

That isn't always easy, or R.L.S. would not elsewhere have spoken of his "great *task* of happiness." Very naturally we all resent those tiresome Pollyannas who foist their cheerfulness upon us regardless of our fate and feelings. Only the whiners and the grumblers are harder to bear with. And those spoiled children of privilege who waste the joys they have by not knowing they have them.

But look around you at some others! Every day I meet them, men and women whom I know to have such trials or disappointments or poverty of opportunity that I marvel at their faces. They are not only brave; they are getting some joy out of life. Such people, I think, improve the climate of our world. They put heart in others to shoulder gallantly the great duty of happiness.

So, lifting one another's spirit, we can get through even our times of trouble. We will not miss the chances of pleasure in a sunset or the face of a friend at the door. And to those faithful in this daily duty of happiness may a rewarding Providence vouchsafe many an unexpected moment of real delight!

Blessed Boomerang

BY

MAURICE CHEVALIER

COMEDIAN

"The days that make us happy make us wise."
—JOHN MASEFIELD

PEOPLE ARE ALL THE TIME asking me one question: "How do you always manage to be so cheerful?"

Of course I do not always feel gay. If I did I would be what you call "slap-happy." But immediately when I sense an audience responding to the gaiety I am trying to give out, I feel gaiety coming back to me. It is like a boomerang—a blessed boomerang.

This works not only for the performer. It is a good game anybody can play.

A man goes to his office. He is grumpy, growls a greeting to his secretary. She may have awakened spirited and jaunty, but right away the ugliness is contagious. Or, in reverse, he comes in whistling. Maybe he has picked a flower from his garden for his buttonhole as he hurried to catch his train. He extends a merry greeting, it boomerangs. The office brightens.

There are targets everywhere. Just take aim and let go with good cheer.

I like to try it out on bus drivers in big cities. They are a worried lot. People ask them long and involved questions, usually about how to get some place in the opposite direction. So board a bus, give a greeting. One time it did not work. I was not in a good mood. My approach, or rather my aim, was poor. The driver snarled, whether in pain or indifference I do not know. Then I transferred to another bus. This time I threw out the greeting with urgency and determination. My greeting was returned, wrapped in a pleasant smile. I got off that bus revived.

The business of getting back something for what you give appeals to my practical French nature, especially when the "something" benefits you so much. It is what they call in business a high rate of return.

So, Happy Hunting—or perhaps I should say Happy Boomeranging!

EDITOR'S NOTE: *For the story of King Vidor's discovery of this same truth, see the next page.*

The Looking Glass

BY

KING VIDOR

PRODUCER AND DIRECTOR

"The world is a looking glass and gives back to every man the reflection of his own face."
—WILLIAM MAKEPEACE THACKERAY

I HAD TO LIVE a long time before I found the courage to admit to myself that we—all of us—make our own world.

The realization came to me in a very simple way. Though I am a Californian, I make frequent trips to New York, and I had decided that all New York cab drivers were impatient, bad-tempered or hated their jobs. And hotel employees and railroad personnel were the same. I found them all difficult to get along with.

Then one day in New York I came upon the words from Thackeray quoted above. The very same day when a cabbie and I were snarling at one another, this thought occurred to me: "Could this whole situation be the result of my own thinking and outlook?"

I began to live Thackeray's idea and soon it became a part of me. The result: On my next trip East, I encountered not one unpleasant taxi driver, elevator operator or employee! Had New York changed or had I? The answer was clear.

To abandon excuses for one's own shortcomings is like journeying to a distant land where everything is new and strange. Here you can't continue to blame someone or something else for failures or difficulties; you have to assume the responsibility for them yourself. Of course, outside pressures do influence our lives, but they don't control them. To assume they do is sheer evasion—it's so easy to say, "It's not my fault!"

Since that day in New York I've come to believe that this idea is the basis of all human relationships. It doesn't matter whether it is your neighbors, your mother-in-law or the people of a foreign nation. The quickest way to correct the other fellow's attitude is to correct your own.

Try it. It works. And it adds immeasurably to the fun of meeting people and being alive.

Find the Key Word

BY

MARGARET BLAIR JOHNSTONE

MINISTER OF THE UNION CONGREGATIONAL
CHURCH, GROTON AND WEST GROTON, MASS.

"Give us courage and gaiety and the quiet mind . . ."
—ROBERT LOUIS STEVENSON

WE WERE in no mood for games when we walked into the classroom at the divinity school. But here we found this line from Stevenson's famous Family Prayer copied on the blackboard, and over it was written "Find the key word."

As student ministers in charge of churches, most of us had been burning the candle at both ends, cramming for comprehensive exams which would determine whether our seven years' professional training was total waste.

"What a time to preach—even about courage!" one man said.

"Quiet mind," muttered another. "Mine's quiet all right. The trouble is, it's paralyzed."

The door opened and in came the professor. "Good morning!" said he, and he surveyed our gloomy ranks. Evidently spotting the glummest, he said, "And how are you this fine morning, Miss Blair?"

"Who—me?" I suddenly came to. "Why—why I'm fine."

"You are! Well, then, why don't you notify your face?"

When we all stopped laughing, we knew the key word. Generated by gaiety we found both courage and calm to take us through the hours we had dreaded. Ever since, in moments of crisis I've found it helps to remember the key word.

EDITOR'S NOTE: *For the complete Family Prayer, see page* 184.

Don't Sneer at Nonsense

BY

JIMMY DURANTE

COMEDIAN

"A little nonsense now and then
Is relished by the wisest men."
—ANONYMOUS

THE OTHER NIGHT, after a very tough day at the studio, I try to get out of a dinner date. I say I'm too tired and grumpy to be good company. But the people insist I've got to show up anyway, since the lamb chops are already in the skillet. So I finally give in.

No sooner do I get in the door when my host says, "Jimmy, dinner's not quite ready and little Clara has been waiting for you to read to her before she goes to sleep." That's just what I need! In the mood I'm in, I'm supposed to go through a bedtime-story session with a four-year-old. But I am trapped, so I go upstairs and take the book the kid gives me and I start to read to her.

I soon get quite a surprise. It's been a long time since I read the wonderful nonsense about the Walrus that cries as he carves the oysters, the Elephant that plays the fife, the Pobble who has no toes, the Owl and the Pussycat which went to sea in a beautiful pea-green boat. I am soon getting as big a kick out of it as the little girl!

When I come downstairs I am all covered with smiles and ready to leap into those lamb chops. And it gets me to thinking, too—which is a feat in itself, folks. I think, Jimmy, nonsense is your stock in trade, but maybe you don't realize how healthy it is off the job.

Maybe there's nobody who is smart and wise enough to do without a little nonsense. Maybe it's even more important than ever these days, when the headlines are not the happiest which I ever read, to have a sort of safety valve.

When we were all kids, we grew up with nonsense as a sort of a friend. And I figure the guy who says to himself, "I've outgrown that sort of stuff," must be a pretty lonely guy.

Nothing Is Wasted

BY

A. P. HERBERT

NOTED BRITISH HUMORIST

"Nothing is wasted."
—E. V. LUCAS

THAT FINE FELLOW, friend and writer, E. V. Lucas, gave me the above saying. If I complained that *Punch* had rejected the funniest article that mortal man had written, he would say, "You'll use it somewhere, someday. Nothing is wasted." Sure enough, very often those thoughts I was so fond of did emerge much later, in a novel, play or speech; and I was glad that they had not appeared before.

In 1935 I went mad and into the House of Commons, interrupting, suspending, for fourteen years, what looked like a promising career as a novelist. E. V. Lucas, then my publisher, disapproved; but he still said, "It's all right—nothing is wasted." I did not trespass into Parliament with any personal aim. If anyone does what he sincerely feels to be a public service, "nothing is wasted" is evidently right. But there is more. I did fall behind in the professional race. Other men went on writing books while I was preparing, making or listening to speeches, drafting amendments, or simply sitting in the smoking room of the House of Commons.

Yet in those fourteen years I learned so much about men and affairs that—even in the material account—I feel the time was not wasted. I should say the same of some (not all) of my nine years in uniform.

But this, you say, is just the egotistical stuff of a writer to whom all experience is "copy." No. It applies to you. After all, it is only another form of "Cast your bread upon the waters . . ." As you sit by the sick bed, or wearily attend committees, or teach the young to add, or mow the lawn, or wash the dishes, or do crossword puzzles, or do any of a thousand things that seem to you, or to your friends, a "waste of time," say to yourself, "Nothing is wasted," and be comforted.

To you, to others, may be given, at any moment, some new glimpse or understanding of life, perhaps some new material wealth. The next time you shave, or go to that dismal committee, you may think of something that will save the world. Your dutiful letters to your aunt may some day be preserved in the British Museum. The author of those little articles in the London *Times* about "Mrs. Miniver" never guessed they would be made into a famous film.

Go on with your laughable hobbies, your dull duties, and your unknown kindnesses, and say, now and then, "Nothing is wasted." The doctrine helps the conscience, too. I have just lost money at the races; I am muttering sadly, "Nothing is wasted." I hope it is true.

3

When You're Down

Failure Isn't Fatal

BY

THE REVEREND JAMES KELLER, M.M.

FOUNDER AND DIRECTOR OF THE CHRISTOPHERS
AUTHOR OF "YOU CAN CHANGE THE WORLD"

"Never despair. But if you do, work on in despair."
—EDMUND BURKE

TOO OFTEN, it seems to me, people lose their courage in facing life because of past failures or fear that they may fail in the future.

One good way to cure such fears is to remember the story of a man who actually built a lifetime of accomplishments out of defeats. The following litany of failures that punctuated his life throughout thirty years is a living and eloquent example of the successful use of defeat in achieving victory. Abraham Lincoln's record is as follows:

Lost job 1832.

Defeated for legislature 1832.

Failed in business 1833.
Elected to legislature 1834.
Sweetheart died 1835.
Had nervous breakdown 1836.
Defeated for Speaker 1838.
Defeated for nomination for Congress 1843.
Elected to Congress 1846.
Lost renomination 1848.
Rejected for land officer 1849.
Defeated for Senate 1854.
Defeated for nomination for Vice-President 1856.
Again defeated for Senate 1858.
Elected President 1860.

Lincoln's deep conviction that God had given him a mission to fulfill accounted in no small way for his deep humility and ability to push on in the face of difficulties and failures that would have discouraged most people.

His abiding faith was well summed up in this comment which he made after becoming President: "God selects His own instruments, and sometimes they are queer ones; for instance, He chose me to steer the ship through a great crisis."

You, too, in God's providence can be an instrument in bringing His love, truth and peace to a world in urgent need of it.

And with Abraham Lincoln, you too can learn to say, "With God's help I shall not fail."

Meet Trouble as a Friend

BY

ISABEL LEIGHTON

EDITOR OF "THE ASPIRIN AGE"

"Trouble makes us one with every human being in the world."

—OLIVER WENDELL HOLMES

A LITTLE MORE than twenty years ago I spent a treasured afternoon with Justice Oliver Wendell Holmes at his Beverly Farms home just north of Boston. Lingering on the threshold as I took my leave, I asked if I might publish some of the typically rugged, earthy observations he had made during our tea together.

With a firmness that belied the gentle smile dancing at the corners of his mouth he replied, "In my more than ninety years I have never allowed myself to be quoted, nor will I revise my pattern at this late date. But write your interview, child, and if, after twenty years from my going, anything I've said still seems to serve a useful purpose, it is yours to do with as you wish."

During those hours, two decades ago, we spoke of many things: the granite on which he built his home—and his life; the barberry bushes he never tired of seeing from his windows; the mystery stories he devoured; and, finally, more dismal matters. Was he not deeply concerned, I asked, over the depression, threats of war and the lack of security in the world? He shook his head indulgently.

"Oh, you young people, you think you've discovered trouble. If you want to live without trouble, you'll have to die young! For if one thing's sure, it's that it's always been with us and always will be.

"Terrifying, you think? Rubbish," he chuckled, "it's never fazed me. Been almost grateful for it at times. Makes us one with every human being in the world—and unless we touch others, we're out of touch with life. You might as well be dead as stop growing and if you're unwilling to feel, yes, feel, deeply, you're only half alive.

"If I had a formula for bypassing trouble, I wouldn't pass it around. Wouldn't be doing anybody a favor. Trouble creates a capacity to handle it. I don't say embrace trouble. That's as bad as treating it as an enemy. But I do say meet it as a friend, for you'll see a lot of it and had better be on speaking terms with it.

"No, trouble isn't the scourge of the world. The world has its ups and downs. So have people, and all the speechifying that breath can produce won't change things or make the millennium come an hour sooner. You can't run away from trouble."

He smiled now more benignly. "Accept it. Don't worry about it. Have faith—and do the needful."

How to Be Mature

BY

DR. HYMAN JUDAH SCHACHTEL

AUTHOR OF "THE REAL ENJOYMENT OF LIFE"

"When it is dark enough, men see the stars."
—RALPH WALDO EMERSON

EMERSON'S WORDS are echoed by an old Oriental proverb, which goes like this: "All sunshine makes a desert." What these sayings express is not an excuse, not a covering up, for the tragic side of life. Rather, I think they speak the truth and give us strength. I think that they go deep into the understanding of the real nature of our lives.

Mature people are made not out of good times but out of bad times. Man's extremity is God's opportunity. It is in a crisis that the best in us comes to the fore. This very age in which we live, which is so turbulent, so confusing, so uncertain, is an anvil upon which God can remake us for the good, for the better.

It is in the encircling gloom that we come to realize the importance of being led by the kindly light of the Eternal One. As Emerson says, it is in the night that we can see the stars which are invisible by day.

What I am asking for is mature outlook, reasonable expectations, a calm and steadfast mind and the patience with which to meet whatever comes with courage and faith in God, instead of with bitterness and resentment.

God's Open Door

BY

DR. A. J. CRONIN

AUTHOR OF "THE CITADEL,"
"A THING OF BEAUTY"

"If God shuts one door, He opens another."
—IRISH PROVERB

THIRTY YEARS AGO, when I was a doctor in London, on the point of moving to a specialist's practice in Harley Street, my health broke down. I was told that I must take a year's rest and that, even so, I might never again be fit to stand the wear and tear of medical life.

What a blow! I liked my work. From the humblest beginnings in a small Welsh mining practice, I had slaved to achieve this objective. And now, on the threshold of success, the door was slammed in my face. My state of mind was such that I could not help voicing bitterness and resentment to my friends.

One of these was an old Irish nun, the Reverend Mother of the Bon Secours, a small order of nursing sisters who occupied a house quite near mine in Westbourne Grove, and who frequently looked after my patients. She heard my outburst in silence, then said:

"You know, Doctor, we have a saying in Ireland, that if God shuts one door, He opens another."

I did not give her remark a second thought and soon after left for my place of exile, a remote district in the West Highlands. Here time hung heavy upon my hands. Suddenly, out of the blue, I had an impulse to write. I began a novel, "Hatter's Castle," and I finished it, packed it up, and sent it to a publisher—who accepted it! Out of all reason, a door had opened. A new career lay before me.

So many of us, meeting with sudden disappointment, misfortune or defeat, raise a cry of anger and resentment against heaven. Why should God do this to us? To be deprived of health, miss the chance of promotion, to lose one's job, these things are hard to bear, and harder perhaps to understand.

Yet we cannot measure Divine Providence by the yardstick of human mentality. What we think an evil may well be for eventual good.

The demands life makes may seem hard at times, yet we ought not to whine. God never takes without giving something in return. Disappointments and troubles are often the instruments with which He fashions us for better things to come.

Life is no straight and easy corridor along which we travel free and unhampered, but a maze of passages, through which we must seek our way, now lost and confused, now checked in a blind alley. But always, if we have faith, God will open a door for us, not perhaps one that we ourselves would ever have thought of, but one that will ultimately prove good for us.

For Lazy People Only

BY

FREDERICK LEWIS ALLEN

EDITOR AND AUTHOR

"Thank God every morning when you get up that you have something to do that day which must be done, whether you like it or not."

—CHARLES KINGSLEY

THERE is a legend at Harvard to the effect that the late Le Baron Russell Briggs, long the beloved dean of the college, once asked a student why he had failed to complete an assignment.

"I wasn't feeling very well, sir," said the student.

"Mr. Smith," said the dean, "I think that in time you may perhaps find that most of the work of the world is done by people who aren't feeling very well."

I have often thought of this remark and wondered whether

Dean Briggs, a man of none too robust health, may not have been feeling a little seedy himself when he uttered it; whether he may not have dragged himself to the office that morning only because he put his responsibilities ahead of his comforts.

The dean knew, I am sure, that there are such things as incapacitating illnesses and that there is such a thing as a sensibly prudent attitude toward one's health. But he also knew that the symptoms of fatigue and of laziness are practically identical; that it is hard to tell the difference between not feeling well and not feeling like doing a hard job; and also that the wise man who has an assignment to complete by Friday has done so much of it on Tuesday and Wednesday that a headache Thursday won't matter much.

He knew the difference between the fellow who plans the jobs he has to do and fits his pleasures into the chinks between them, and the fellow who plans his pleasures and then begins to think of his responsibilities.

Again and again Dean Briggs's remark comes back to me on those dismal mornings when it seems outrageous that anybody should have to settle down to work at nine o'clock. And I start laughing at myself, and presently I feel more like buckling down and doing the thing that has to be done.

Grandma Moses' Medicine

BY

GERALD W. JOHNSON

AUTHOR OF "THIS AMERICAN PEOPLE"

"Then Anna was born, so I had four babies to care for. But we got along very nice till the children got the scarlet fever, that was a hard year but it passed on like all the rest."

—GRANDMA MOSES, in *My Life's History*

THESE TWO SENTENCES constitute Grandma Moses' complete and unabridged account of one of her ninety-two years.

Its brevity, I believe, goes far to explain why Grandma has lived into her tenth decade. She is not inarticulate. She can describe in loving and minute detail, after sixty years, her wedding dress, a Thanksgiving dinner, a practical joke she and another girl played; but about a hard year she found nothing worth remembering except that "it passed on like all the rest."

Nobody can explain genius, so exactly what it is that makes Grandma Moses a magnificent painter no man can tell. But if you want to know why she has remained alert, vigorous, radiantly alive into her nineties, mull over the above bit of philosophy.

Beauty, love, laughter and delight are imperishable memories, but all that is important about hardship is that it passes. How right she is! If we could only remember this truth in the hard years, how many spiritual scars and deformities we should escape, and how much more abundant would life be in the years that are given us!

I Won't Worry

BY

MARY HEMINGWAY

"Worry a little bit every day and in a lifetime you will lose a couple of years. If something is wrong, fix it if you can. But train yourself not to worry. Worry never fixes anything."

—OLE HELGERSON

OLE HELGERSON, who gave me that good counsel, was a Norwegian pioneer farmer who was also engineer on my father's boat in northern Minnesota. His words were in response to some momentous problem of mine when I was ten, but they have traveled with me through the years and proved helpful in every one of them.

"Worrying is just wasting time," Ole had explained. "Like throwing away some good thing." Remembering his admonition and his conscientious care both of his farm and of my father's engines, I have gradually understood that Ole was not recommending heedlessness, or the avoidance of forethought. He was not belittling the profit to be gained from experience or from considered action—"Fix it if you can." Nor would he underestimate the complex tasks of thinking required for charting the strange course of our world.

What Ole started me to learning—I haven't yet mastered it—is the worthlessness of nagging at most problems, or of lingering with them when they are unsolvable. He helped me begin the practice, when something cannot be fixed, of purposefully turning attention to happier enterprises. It has saved me many hours, not only during the war and in emergencies, but in the fascinating process of living each new day. These words were a useful and enduring gift.

EDITOR'S NOTE: *For another version of Ole Helgerson's advice,* *see A Practical Prayer, page 186.*

The Day the Sun Went Out

BY

LOWELL THOMAS

AUTHOR AND WORLD TRAVELER

"I choose to be found doing my duty."
—ABRAHAM DAVENPORT

IN THESE atomic times, when so many people are trembling about the "ultimate disaster," I find that there is a sort of steadying strength in the following story:

It was on May 19, 1780—during the anxious days of our Revolutionary War—that darkness came at noon. The bats flew and chickens roosted. It was some sort of meteorological phenomenon that seemed to bring the day to an end when the sun was at zenith. Panic broke out, and people thought that the end of the world was at hand.

At Hartford, Connecticut, the State Legislature was in session and, when the darkness came at noon, the meeting of the Lower House broke up in alarm. In the State Senate a motion of adjournment was made, so that the legislators could meet the Day of Judgment with whatever courage they could manage to summon.

But the motion was opposed by Abraham Davenport, a Yankee selectman and judge, friend and adviser of George Washington. Abraham Davenport faced the panic about the end of the world with the best of Yankee heart and head.

He arose and addressed his legislative colleagues. "I am against this adjournment," he said. Then he explained with a logic of courage:

"The Day of Judgment," he said, "is either approaching or it is not. If it is not, there is no cause for adjournment. If it is, I choose to be found doing my duty. I wish, therefore, that candles may be brought."

Of course, this was not the only time that people have beheld what seems to be the ultimate disaster. In the past they have trembled in the presence of such nightmares as the invasion of the Huns led by Attila, the Scourge of God, or the rage of plagues like the Black Death, or the predicted end of the world in the year 1000.

But in all history it would be hard to find a better example for our times than the sturdy figure of Abraham Davenport. At a time when we are all haunted by doubts and questions about the possibility of atomic war and trying to decide what course to take, he gives us the only possible answer: *"I choose to be found doing my duty."*

How to Be Sure

BY

MARGARET CULKIN BANNING

NOVELIST AND SHORT-STORY WRITER

"Act as if it were impossible to fail."
—DOROTHEA BRANDE, *Wake Up and Live!*

IN THE DEVOTIONAL classic *Imitation of Christ,* Thomas à Kempis tells the story of a certain person who was so filled with anxiety and fear that he could not bring himself to act. As he wavered back and forth in his uncertainty he thought, Oh, if I only knew such and such, then I should have the courage to persevere.

And presently, wrote Thomas, he heard within himself this answer from God: "And if you did know, what would you do? Do now what you would then do, and you shall be very secure."

This very practical rule of living destroys worry and apprehension about both big and little things. For example, you cannot be sure that a relative or friend will enjoy visiting you—but you would ask him if you were sure. Very well, then—invite him *as if* you were sure! Or, you cannot be sure that your child will distinguish himself if you send him to college, and it is an expensive investment. But send him *as if* you were sure he would do well. Or, you can't be sure that your job will succeed if you put in extra work on it, but how can you satisfy yourself without proceeding *as if* you did know it would succeed?

There are plenty of practical examples in everyone's life; these are only suggestions of how it can help to act "as if." These have proved useful words for me to live by. I've used them many times. The result may not always be what you hope for, but the sense that you have done the best you can to make things work out, and have given opportunity itself a chance, does produce in yourself that inner peace which is the best kind of security.

4

Ways to Success

Start Over

BY

DR. SMILEY BLANTON

AUTHOR OF "LOVE OR PERISH"

"We must think anew—and act anew."
—ABRAHAM LINCOLN

WHEN ABRAHAM LINCOLN wrote these words, he was facing the greatest crisis that this nation has ever endured: the Civil War. He knew that ordinary measures were not enough. "The dogmas of the quiet past," he wrote, "are inadequate to the stormy present. We must think anew, and act anew."

New thought, new action—how simple it sounds and how difficult it is! Most of us tend to be shackled by old habits of thought, by the dogmas of the past. When crisis threatens, it is all too easy to go on acting—or reacting—as we did before.

But great rewards await men and women who can change

the pattern of their thinking to meet new conditions or new challenges. I have proof of this in my own experience. When I first left college, I had no intention of becoming a psychiatrist. I spent three years in dramatic school, then went to Cornell University to teach speech and drama. But two years later, reviewing my life, I decided that, much as I enjoyed teaching, what I really wanted to be was a doctor.

The decision to "act anew" was not easy. I knew that I would be well into my thirties before I had a medical degree, that I could hardly hope to become an established psychiatrist before I was forty. My friends counseled against such a drastic step. I took it anyway. I have never regretted it for an instant.

Today, many of the people who come to me for help are suffering from a kind of rigidity caused by blind adherence to old patterns of thinking and acting. They cannot adapt to changing conditions. They find it so difficult to bend that sometimes they break.

Quite often, in my efforts to help such people, I quote these words of Lincoln. When problems beset us, I tell them —when there seems to be no solution—we must not act rigidly. We must not look at our difficulties from old, habit-worn, outmoded points of view. We must think anew, and with the new thoughts will come the power and the confidence to act anew.

A great American told us this. We should remember his words and try to live by them—as he did.

Make the Minutes Count

BY

M. LINCOLN SCHUSTER

PUBLISHER, EDITOR OF
"A TREASURY OF THE WORLD'S GREAT LETTERS"

"Every minute starts an hour."
—PAUL GANDOLA

THE MOST CREATIVE man I know is over ninety. He is Bernard Berenson, the world-famous art historian and humanist, who has willed to Harvard University his fabulous paintings and his incomparable library in Florence.

The secret of his achievement—and his happiness—is that he has "no time to spare."

When I saw "B.B." last he was still unquenchably young in heart, a supreme master of the greatest art of all—the art of living. This is the art of getting sixty minutes from the hour, twenty-four hours from the day. Never willing merely to add years to his life, he always insists on adding life to his years. He does it by being everlastingly interested in the world around him.

Each minute of his time is dedicated, disciplined, undistracted. In his tenth decade his agenda of unfinished business is more inspiring than ever. At the moment he is working on five books, completing a vast and comprehensive catalogue of the Renaissance—and still enjoying the master fulfillment of getting things done.

In his classically beautiful villa, I Tatti, amidst the olive-crowned, cypress-guarded hills of Tuscany, surrounded by the Giottos and Tintorettos which he has himself discovered and authenticated, he still rules over the Mediterranean realms of scholarship in the visual arts. But not content to be the most famous art critic in the world, he has also a passion to touch life at all points. Rejecting narrow specialization, he has taken all the humanities as his province. That is why he has no time to spare.

When my wife and I saw B.B. on a recent birthday he was, he said, so steeped in "work in progress" that he wanted to stand on the street corner, cap in hand, like a mendicant, begging the idle passers-by for the hours and minutes they were wasting.

Here is an image to remember. It is one which may make you stop and think again, whenever you are tempted to say you're bored or that you have "time to kill." It may help you to remember that the happiest people are generally those who have "no time to spare."

EDITOR'S NOTE: *For more about Paul Gandola, see page 210.*

Make a Mistake

BY

ROBERT HILLYER

PULITZER PRIZE POET

"I intended an Ode, And it turn'd to a Sonnet."
—AUSTIN DOBSON

HOW OFTEN we intend one thing and it turns into another! There is a joke in the Greek anthology about a man who invented a stove that didn't work but served excellently as a wine cooler in summer. The New England eccentric "Lord" Timothy Dexter of Newburyport, Massachusetts, sent a strange cargo of warming pans to the West Indies and made his fortune when the natives discovered that the pans, with their long handles, were perfect for cooking in a hot climate.

Centuries of apparently wasted effort on the part of alchemists not only gave birth to chemistry but also provided a rich storehouse of symbols for philosophy and poetry. Columbus aimed at India and found America. The experience has become proverbial: we aim for the goose and hit the gander.

The same thing happens with cheerful frequency in daily life. A job is lost which, if it had been taken, would have prevented the acceptance of a better one. The wrong book comes home from the library and opens a whole new field of interest. I know of a student in college who wandered into the wrong classroom and became so interested in the subject being discussed there that he pursued it and made it his career. I need scarcely add that, being so absent-minded, he became a famous professor.

It is better to wait and see what happens than to be discouraged. It should take the edge off disappointment to remember that half the things that go wrong surprise us by turning out all right

Raise Your Sights

BY

DR. ROGER BANNISTER

FIRST MAN TO RUN THE FOUR-MINUTE MILE

"Now understand me well. Out of every fruition of success, no matter what, comes forth something to make a new effort necessary."

—WALT WHITMAN

RECENTLY at White City Stadium, London (with thirty thousand spectators), I looked down on four of the world's finest milers. My job as television commentator was to give TV viewers their share in the drama, and this time the significance of the drama went far beyond the world of sports.

A great mile is like a play. More than any other sporting event it has the unities of time, place and action. The basic struggle is physical, but the real clash is one of personality.

We ourselves take sides. And the villains of the piece are the weather and the track.

But that evening the air was still and the running surface good. The heroes were Ron Delany, an Olympic champion; Stanislav Jungwirth, a 1,500-meter ace; Britain's carefree four-minute miler, Derek Ibbotson; and his compatriot, Ken Wood.

Ibbotson created a race that came as near to perfection as a mile can. In a flashing finish he carried three other runners through the four-minute barrier for the first time in the history of sport.

That was a far cry from the first modern mile back in 1886, when Walter George, wearing knee-length tubular shorts, and in spite of extra wind resistance from a flowing mustache, negotiated the mile in four minutes, twelve and three quarters seconds—a record that remained for thirty-seven years until Paavo Nurmi pared it by two seconds in 1923.

Thirty-one years later the first four-minute mile was run. I was lucky enough to be the one to do it. Now, in only three brief years, this time had been broken on twenty-six occasions by sixteen runners. What was the reason?

It cannot be explained solely by improved training methods, though the technique of interval running (sprint, jog, walk, sprint) has made a great contribution. We forget that four minutes was merely an arbitrary time, fast perhaps, but still only a time. The barrier for spectators and runners was a psychological, not a physical, one; they failed to fix their sights high enough. But now, finally, the magic of a four-minute limit has lost its hypnotic power.

What the next record will be is anybody's guess, but what happened on that particular day in London is a reminder that we should never be hypnotized by any mental limitation. We can always raise our sights.

Forget the Joneses

BY

DOROTHY VAN DOREN

EDITOR AND AUTHOR

"We should have much peace if we would not busy ourselves with the sayings and doings of others."
—THOMAS À KEMPIS

THESE WORDS do not mean, I believe, that we should withdraw into our shells and shut the world out; they do not mean Mind Your Own Business; they do not mean Keep Mum, Chum. I think they mean Don't Knock Yourself Out Trying to Keep Up with the Joneses!

The family next door has a new car. Yours is ten years old. Does it worry you? The girl who works at the desk in front of you has just bought a new summer outfit, and besides, she has naturally curly hair. Do you envy her? There are three men who ride to work with you every day. One has just been promoted, one has finished paying off the mortgage on his house, one has married a charming young wife. Do you lie awake wondering why these good things haven't happened to you?

We should have much peace, says Thomas, if we could stop worrying—"busying ourselves"—about other people and concentrate on ourselves. We are our own special problem—I am my problem, you are yours. Each of us has his own hopes, ambitions, talents, skills. Not only is it our job to develop these talents and skills to their fullest in order to realize these ambitions and hopes, but it is, as Thomas à Kempis reminds us, our peace also.

Be good, says the old saw, and you will be happy. Thomas is at once more realistic and more specific; most people, he knows, are neither good nor happy. But if we stop envying our neighbor's latest piece of good fortune, whatever it may be, and concentrate on developing our own talents, we shall have taken the first step toward inner peace.

Go to Work

BY

WILFRED FUNK

AUTHOR, EDITOR AND PUBLISHER

"Genius is the capacity for taking infinite pains."
—THOMAS CARLYLE

THE OTHER DAY my children were asking me about the word "genius." They thought that it must be very pleasant to be a genius. They imagined, for example, that a poet just lay on the grass under a tree, looked up through the green and shimmering sunlit leaves, then suddenly seized paper and pencil and in a frenetic frenzy of inspiration wrote his immortal lines. Very nice. Very easy.

At this point, I began to gather definitions of genius by the geniuses themselves. Here are several from my collection:

Said Paderewski: *"Before I was a genius, I was a drudge."*

Said Flaubert: *"Genius, in the phrase of Buffon, is only long patience. Work."*

Said Michelangelo: *"If people knew how hard I work to get my mastery it wouldn't seem so wonderful after all."*

Said Carlyle: *"Genius is the capacity for taking infinite pains."*

Said Alexander Hamilton: *"All of the genius I have is merely the fruit of labor."*

How often people have said to me that they would like to write, or paint, or play an instrument "if only they had the talent." Yet I have never discovered a genius who spoke of talent. Or even of inspiration. Only brutal work.

So, if you or I or my children don't succeed, might it not be more fitting to blame it, perhaps, on a measure of laziness rather than lack of talent?

Pick a Hero

BY

JOHN FOSTER DULLES

LAWYER AND STATESMAN

"Seeing we also are compassed about with so great a cloud of witnesses . . . let us run with patience the race that is set before us."

—HEBREWS 12:1

MOST OF US do not have time to sit down and work out in detail just what it is we believe or just what life is all about. Our days are so full of things to be done that there is not much time for abstract thinking. But the danger then is that life becomes purposeless, haphazard and dreary.

The Apostle Paul suggested a good solution in the quotation above. He had reviewed Hebrew history in about thirty short dramatic paragraphs, recalling the names of men and women of the past who had found it possible to do notable deeds and to bear cruel hardships because they had the inspiration of a faith in something better and higher than themselves. Then he appealed to his generation to live as though they, in turn, were running a race which these heroic forebears were watching.

That is a good rule for Americans to apply. We differ sharply about the merits and demerits of living Americans, but as time goes by certain figures of our past emerge as having an heroic quality. There would not be complete agreement, but if we were writing a short American history, like the short Hebrew history that Paul wrote, most of us would mention such Americans as Washington, Jefferson, Hamilton, Nathan Hale, John Paul Jones, Lincoln, Jane Addams, Booker Washington and the Unknown Soldier.

Whatever the list, all those we named would, like those on Paul's list, be men and women who struggled and sacrificed in a deep faith that life had a purpose beyond their own material self-satisfaction.

When we attribute greatness to these Americans of the past, we are, in reality and largely unconsciously, making a standard of conduct for ourselves. The next step is for us to make our own lives into the kind of effort which we think our chosen heroes would applaud. Then the life of each individual takes on dignity, worth and purpose, and the total effect is to transform the nation into a dynamic force for righteousness.

Act the Part

BY

CHARLES SCHNEE

PRODUCER AND WRITER

"Always act the part—and you can become whatever you wish to become!"

—MAX REINHARDT

ONCE AS A schoolboy journalist interviewing Reinhardt, I had the impressive experience of watching the great Austrian producer conduct a rehearsal for his New York production of *The Miracle.* I heard him address to a player the words quoted above, and I thought he was speaking only in terms of professional acting. But now I know that his words also apply to any individual in any walk of life.

That's why I say: Act the part wherever you are. Select the qualities you most admire—and then act as if you had them.

Believe me, there is nothing cynical about this advice. It does not mean faking, or bluffing, or putting on airs. Rather it means setting yourself some good, high standards and living up to them. Then, even if you don't have the qualities to start with, you'll stand a good chance of attracting them to you.

Reinhardt himself played a role—and he played it to the hilt. He always took with him an aura of greatness, of authority, of genius.

I have known many a plain-looking woman who became a more beautiful woman—just by acting like a beautiful, graceful, self-possessed woman.

I have known men who climbed to leadership by picking that role and acting like leaders.

Yes—act the part! I believe in this rule. I believe that if we try acting like better friends and neighbors, we will end up being better friends and neighbors, too.

Take a Chance

BY

WALT DISNEY

MOTION PICTURE PRODUCER

> *"In the lexicon of youth . . . there is no such word as fail!"*
>
> —EDWARD BULWER-LYTTON

I WONDER how many times these sturdy old words have been used in graduation speeches each year. They take me back to my own high-school days, when I had my first pair of white flannel trousers and the world ahead held no heartbreak or fear.

Certainly we have all had this confidence at one time in our lives, though most of us lose it as we grow older. Perhaps, because of my work, I've been lucky enough to retain a shred of this youthful quality. But sometimes, as I look back on how tough things were, I wonder if I'd go through it again. I hope I would.

When I was about twenty-one, I went broke for the first time. I slept on chair cushions in my "studio" in Kansas City and ate cold beans out of a can. But I took another look at my dream and set out for Hollywood.

Foolish? Not to a youngster. An older person might have had too much "common sense" to do it. Sometimes I wonder if "common sense" isn't another way of saying "fear." And "fear" too often spells failure.

In the lexicon of youth there is no such word as "fail." Remember the story about the boy who wanted to march in the circus parade? When the show came to town, the bandmaster needed a trombonist, so the boy signed up. He hadn't marched a block before the fearful noises from his horn caused two old ladies to faint and a horse to run away. The bandmaster demanded, "Why didn't you tell me you couldn't play the trombone?" And the boy said, "How did I know? I never tried before!"

Many years ago, I might have done just what that boy did. Now I'm a grandfather and have a good many gray hairs and what a lot of people would call common sense. But if I'm no longer young in age, I hope I stay young enough in spirit never to fear failure—young enough still to take a chance and march in the parade.

Don't Wait Too Long

BY

GENERAL OMAR N. BRADLEY

FORMER CHIEF OF STAFF, U.S. ARMY

"Postpone not your life."
—RALPH WALDO EMERSON

THERE IS NOTHING that is easier than putting aside a letter or a decision and saying, "Let it answer itself."

It is true that a good many letters and problems do. But the fact remains that life cannot be lived on that premise. There is always a time when we have to face up to responsibility. As Emerson put it in the words above, "Postpone not your life."

In battle, the lives of men and the success of an entire campaign may depend on the commander's decision. Where time permits, the commander makes a very careful analysis and estimate of the situation. However, time does not always permit him to wait and to vacillate in making the decision.

It has often been said that a "second best" decision quickly made and vigorously carried out is better than the "best" decision if it is too long in being arrived at or halfheartedly carried out. It is better for the commander to keep so well informed of the facts as they happen that he can, if necessary, make quick decisions. There may be no time for postponement.

In war or peace the naked fact remains the same. We are given one life, we have one span to live it. We can wait for circumstances to make up their minds or we can decide to act, and, in acting, live.

When I was a boy finishing high school in Missouri, I wanted to go to college, but I was going to have to stay out for a year and work to earn the money. While I was waiting I heard about West Point. I could go to school there, learn to be an officer and have a career.

I knew nothing about West Point and I could have waited and tried college for a year and then made up my mind, but I didn't. I thought about it one night and the next day I told my mother, "I am going to try."

It seemed crystal clear to me at eighteen. It seems crystal clear to me now. When I retired from active duty in the Army I was offered a job in a totally new field. I could have waited and thought about it, but instead I told my wife, "I am going to try."

Look at it, size it up, but don't "postpone your life" just because you can't make up your mind.

Dare to Be Different!

BY

VICE ADMIRAL
HYMAN G. RICKOVER

PIONEER OF THE ATOMIC SUBMARINE

"Whoso would be a man must be a non-conformist"
—RALPH WALDO EMERSON

THE ANCIENT LOCRIANS in Greece gave freedom of speech to all citizens—though at a cost which many must have considered too high. At public meetings, anyone could stand up and argue for changes in law or custom, on one condition. A rope was placed around his neck before he began to speak and if what he said did not meet with public approval, he was forthwith hanged.

Here in America, it would indeed be tragic if democracy deteriorated into mass tyranny over the unconventional individual. Democracy and equality do not require that we deny to the minority of people with creative minds the right to use them in their own way and to their fullest potential. People who use their minds successfully ought not to be expected to pretend they are just like everybody else.

We should then lose the diversity from which spring all great ideas; we should rob ourselves of the precious quality that distinguishes man from all other orders—his determination to think for himself, to be different.

Meet Luck Halfway

BY

GEORGE AND HELEN PAPASHVILY

AUTHORS OF "ANYTHING CAN HAPPEN" AND "THANKS TO NOAH"

"God tries you with a little, to see what you'd do with a lot."

—ANONYMOUS

NEWS TRAVELS FAST in the country. Ever since a poor-as-a-church-mouse family in our end of the township came in for a large and unexpected sum of money last month all our party-line and crossroad conversations have been variations on a single theme:

"How come Charlie and Belle were so lucky—why not us? What's Charlie got I don't have? What's Belle deserve that you don't?"

Envy rose like a mist and the air teemed with self-pity—

until our very oldest neighbor came home from a visit and cleared the atmosphere.

She was delighted to hear the great news, but not surprised. "Just what I always expected," she said. "I could have told you it was bound to happen. Remember when Charlie didn't have a cent of cash for the hospital fund—he gave two days of his time hauling stone? Belle's the same way. She never waits until that 'someday' when she can do the Big Thing for you—she does all the little things when you need them most. She can be as happy—and a lot more generous—with a package of petunia seeds than some women with a hothouse full of gardenias.

"Even little Chuck—while he saved money for his accordion, he learned the harmonica. So they'll make good use of all that's come to them. I've often thought maybe God tries you with a little first, just to see if you'd know what to do with a lot."

5

Some Virtues

Bravery

BY

GENERAL MAXWELL D. TAYLOR

CHIEF OF STAFF, U.S. ARMY

"He either fears his fate too much,
Or his deserts are small,
That dares not put it to the touch,
To gain or lose it all."
—MARQUIS OF MONTROSE

THESE LINES from the seventeenth-century Marquis of Montrose have special meaning for me because of the way in which I first heard them.

The greatest military operation of history was the Allied invasion of Normandy in June 1944. Probably no other operation ever received such careful planning and meticulous attention to its smallest requirements. For months the training areas, airfields and ports of Great Britain hummed with the activity of soldiers, sailors and airmen. Important phases of the invasion plan were rehearsed in great maneuvers which reproduced with all possible realism the conditions anticipated in combat.

As D Day approached, the senior commanders assembled their principal subordinates for a final review of the plans. The largest conference of this kind was held in St. Paul's School in London under the monitorship of Field Marshal Montgomery. Here the Allied commanders of all the services consulted together and verified the readiness of their preparations.

After a long day of earnest discussions, as the meeting was about to adjourn, Marshal Montgomery arose and gave a final address in which he expressed his confidence in the success of this great enterprise. In closing, he commended to us the words of Montrose I have quoted. They were with me on D Day in Normandy and have been with me ever since as a spur to decisive action when the cards are down.

I stress the importance of the context, because in themselves these words might be taken simply as poetic counsel to a rash willingness to "shoot the works." But with the background of our careful preparations for Normandy, they become a rejection of fear of failure after every preparation has been made and every contingency anticipated.

Assuming such preparations, these words say that there are times in the lives of both men and nations when we must be willing to risk much in order to win much. They are a counsel against timidity and for the bold recognition of those great moments when we must be prepared to "let the chips fall where they may." In these troubled times we can exert effective leadership only if it is apparent to the whole world that there are certain things so important that, regardless of hazard, we dare to put all to the test, as becomes a people whose deserts are large.

Boldness

BY

JAMES A. MICHENER

AUTHOR OF "TALES OF THE SOUTH PACIFIC"

"Behold the turtle: He makes progress only when he sticks his neck out."

—JAMES BRYANT CONANT

THESE LIVELY words of a famous scientist and educator have special meaning for me.

In 1944 I was stuck on a remote island in the South Pacific. To kill time I decided to write a book. Then I remembered the cold facts: The chances against anyone's publishing a first book are ninety-five to one; for each book that is finally published, ninety-five unsuccessful ones are written. But I decided to stick my neck out and go ahead.

Then I learned two more facts. If a man hasn't written a book by the time he's thirty-five years old, chances are he never will. And I was nearing forty. Even worse, I was not writing a novel but a book of short stories. A friend warned me, "Nobody publishes books of short stories any more." Even so, I still decided to stick my neck out. And it was then I found I was in good company.

When the book appeared, it seemed as if the prophecies of doom had been correct. My work caused little comment and would have died unknown except that Orville Prescott, a newspaper book reviewer, took a chance on a beginning writer and reported that he had liked the stories.

Later, a group of literary critics studied the book and pointed out, "It's not a novel, it's not about America, and common sense says it's not eligible for the Pulitzer Prize." Nevertheless they awarded it the prize and so brought the book to the world's attention.

In Hollywood, Kenneth MacKenna, who reads books for the movies, tried to persuade his company to make a movie out of *Tales of the South Pacific,* but the experts replied, "No dramatic possibilities." So MacKenna stuck his neck out and brought the book to the attention of Richard Rodgers and Oscar Hammerstein II, who did likewise.

When Broadway heard that R & H planned a musical called *South Pacific,* wiseacres cried, "Have you heard their screwy idea? The romantic lead is gonna be a man past fifty. An opera singer named Ezio Pinza!" You know what happened next!

You can understand why I like people who stick their necks out.

Courage

BY

BARBARA BEL GEDDES

ACTRESS

"You've got to keep fighting—you've got to risk your life every six months to stay alive."

—ELIA KAZAN

I EXPECT I'm not the best person to give advice about life, since most of my friends think I'm crazy anyhow. But I bet I'm having more fun than they are, and the little quote above has a great deal to do with it.

Elia Kazan never said it to me personally, though he directed me in several shows. I ran across it in a magazine, of all places. I was out in Hollywood on a contract that was really plush for a girl of my experience. But I wasn't feeling too happy about it. Some of the pictures they'd cast me in were pretty dreadful. A couple of them have already been released for TV—they were that bad.

In any case, I read the quote in a story about Kazan, and it got under my skin so much that I cut it out and stuck it in the corner of my dressing-room mirror. I thought, here I've got an easy life, but is it really living? A few weeks later I managed to get myself out of that contract, and there isn't a doubt in my mind that the quote made me do it.

Everybody said I was committing suicide, but I lived—and wonderfully. I went back to Broadway and got a new lease on life.

I know it's supposed to be wise to think of tomorrow, but sometimes I think there's too much worrying about security in the world today. If you fret about tomorrow so much that you don't dare live today, don't dare get out of a rut when you have a chance, then how wise are you?

I don't mean that everyone should chuck his job and head for the South Sea Isles. But you don't have to risk that much to really live. The poorest man in America can afford to wake up some fine morning and say, "The devil with the shop today—I'm going fishing." Or the most harried housewife can say, "Let the beds and dishes take care of themselves for once. I'm going out in the sun!" Just risking your life that much can give you the wonderful feeling of living today.

Serenity

BY

I. A. R. WYLIE

MAGAZINE WRITER AND NOVELIST

"Heavenly Father, give us serenity to accept what cannot be changed, courage to change what should be changed and wisdom to know one from the other."

A CARD on which this centuries-old prayer is printed is on my work desk, facing me. It has been there for many years. I have carried it round the world with me, through the vicissitudes of a fairly eventful life. Since by nature I am not serene—like most of us, courageous only in spots—and rarely wise, I have often needed it. It has stood me in good stead on many occasions.

The first time that I remember was, of all odd places, under a kitchen table in the basement of my London home.

(The kitchen table, in those early war days, was the average Londoner's dugout.) Overhead, through the merciless light of a hunter's moon, antiaircraft shells screamed viciously but ineffectively. With a fearful, sickening thud an aerial torpedo struck nearby. Through a moment's appalled silence I could hear the hiss of descending rubble.

It was my first encounter with full-scale death and destruction. I was on the verge of a futile panic when, like a strong hand, reaching across the years, that old prayer took hold of me. I felt as though I had been lifted out of a black, demoniac pit onto a high serene place of refuge. What would be would be. I was helpless to avert it. All that mattered—all that lay in my power—was the manner of my acceptance.

Serenity isn't gray resignation. It's a golden, smiling quality. To possess it is to be armed against what, I suppose, is the hardest-to-accept, most unchangeable fact of life—the process of leaving it. I pray daily, not to be resigned to old age, not to yield supinely to its limitations, but to accept with a cheerful serenity what remains to me of accomplishment and experience.

It is said that this prayer was prayed for the first time by a soldier. If so he must have been a good soldier who knew when to fight, what to fight for and eventually how to die. Across the centuries I pay him this debt of gratitude.

EDITOR'S NOTE: *For the source of this prayer, see page 186.*

Modesty

BY

KATHRYN HULME

AUTHOR OF "THE NUN'S STORY"

"Do good, and disappear."
—GENEVIEVE HENNET DE GOUTEL

I FIRST HEARD these words years ago from the dedicated woman whose story I was one day to write. She told me that the words came from the diary of Genevieve Hennet de Goutel, a heroic French nurse who died in World War I. They were painted in large Gothic letters over the door of a ward in the convent hospital in Belgium where she received her training.

The sense of the saying was immediately apparent. It's this: When you give something, say something or do something helpful to a fellow man, you don't stand around waiting to collect your pound of gratitude—the shy smile, the stumbling words of thanks or, worse still, the tears which sometimes come when great weights of trouble are suddenly lifted. You simply give, say or do—and disappear.

It sounds easy. But it is very difficult; it is as if one has a gaunt and rapacious wolf inside one, hungry for gratitude.

It's true that our charitable contributions often have to be identified, for tax or other reasons. But that isn't always the case. Last summer in the Jackson Hole country of Wyoming, I visited a small log cabin church which had a list of its needs posted in the vestibule. A contribution of a few dollars would build a closet for the holy vestments. I had some cash with me, but instead of just dropping it in the box, I put it in an envelope with my name and address so that there could be no mistake as to which passing tourist had been touched by the simple appeal. In due course came a letter from the grateful father of that forlorn parish, blessing me for my donation. The letter shamed me then and still does.

But beyond that, it robbed me of the true inner happiness which is the greatest of all rewards—and which comes to you when you simply "do good and disappear."

Enthusiasm

BY

SAMUEL GOLDWYN

FAMOUS HOLLYWOOD PRODUCER

"Nothing great was ever achieved without enthusiasm."

—RALPH WALDO EMERSON

EMERSON was certainly right—but not right enough. For enthusiasm is the key not only to the achievement of great things but to the accomplishment of anything that is worth while.

Enthusiasm is a wonderful word. But more, it is a wonderful feeling. It is a way of life. It is a magic spark that transforms "being" into "living." It makes hard work easy—and enjoyable. There is no better tonic for depression, no greater elixir for whatever happens to be wrong at the moment, than enthusiasm.

No person who is enthusiastic about his work has anything to fear from life. All the opportunities in the world—and they are as plentiful today as ever despite what some people say—are waiting to be grasped by the people who are in love with what they are doing.

For as long as I can remember, whatever I was doing at the time was the most important thing in the world to me. Today I look forward to my next picture with the same degree of excitement and anticipation and enthusiasm with which I went into my very first production.

I have found enthusiasm for work and life to be the most precious ingredient in any recipe for successful living. And the greatest feature of this ingredient is that it is available to everyone—within himself.

Confidence

BY

KONRAD ADENAUER

FEDERAL GERMAN CHANCELLOR

"Lift where you stand."
—EDWARD EVERETT

MOST OF US, in moments of fatigue or discouragement, have taken a look at our daily task and wondered, "What does it really matter?" Precisely at those moments we should tell ourselves what my lifetime has taught me is the one true answer: "I shall keep doing the job, for I matter a great deal."

Let me counsel young people who are ambitious that they can best get ahead by making themselves important in the job at hand. Then they will not have to look for the next higher job—it will be offered to them. In all humility, I was much too busy being mayor of my well-loved city of Cologne to waste time dreaming that some day my countrymen might ask me to be their Chancellor. Yet that day came.

When the world seems large and complex, we need to remember that great world ideals all begin in some home neighborhood. I doubt, for example, that the men of the Middle Ages who built Germany's famed free cities guessed how high they were building. They simply did the job at hand. Yet now we have their traditions of liberal self-government as a model for our free republic; those city planners set an example that has outlasted kaisers and dictators.

So history shows us that our moments of discouragement can become the moments for our new starts. When we put inspiration into raising our family, or do the shop work better than required, or make our town a model for others, then our influence spreads in widening circles. We are each more important than we think.

Imagination

BY

MARY MARTIN

"Every wish is like a prayer to God."
—ELIZABETH BARRETT BROWNING

IF I HAD the magic gift of Tinker Bell, I'd flit into the minds of my friends and leave this prescription for happiness: Stop the habit of wishful thinking and start the habit of thoughtful wishes. I would sweep away all those dreary office desk signs that say "Think" for another batch that shout "Wish!" Wishes are thoughts vibrant with life and eager for action. They have the power to produce light and beauty.

Personally I am almost afraid of the power in a wish, so many of mine have come true. As a little girl in Weatherford, Texas, I had five giant wishes. First, I wanted to fly—not aviator style, but like an angel. Second, as I emerged from pigtails, I wanted to marry a "wonderful guy" and have two children. I also wanted to sing to the world. I hankered to live in a house on a tree-covered hill in some faraway land. And, above all, I yearned to perform on a London stage with my idol, Noel Coward, whom I had seen at the local movie house in *The Scoundrel.*

My wish to fly stuck hauntingly with me into adulthood. At least once a week I'd dream I was airborne under my own power. One night I had a vivid dream of flying into New York through the Holland Tunnel. How I managed to sail over the long stream of trucks and cars, without hitting the ceiling, only Freud knows.

Soon after that I received a telegram offering me the role of Peter Pan on Broadway. During its long run I did a heap of "flying" angel style. And the funny thing is that never have I dreamed of flying again.

One night after my première in *One Touch of Venus,* several years ago, I was dining late at an intimate, dimly lit restaurant near the theater. A man I had never met emerged from the shadows, passed my table, bent down and kissed my forehead.

"You were wonderful," he said.

It was Noel Coward. Four years later I went to London to star in *Pacific 1860,* a musical he wrote especially for his worshiper from Weatherford.

The blessing of the "wonderful guy" and the two children has also come my way. And we've bought a house on a hillside in Brazil where we can all be together. Nowadays, I watch my wishes like a hawk.

What is true of me applies to everyone. It's a wonderful custom to extend best wishes to our friends at New Year's. But, more important, let's be sure to extend best wishes to ourselves—wish them to ourselves with all our heart and strive toward them with all our might.

If you're willing to do that, select your wishes with care. For they have an uncanny way of coming true!

Patience

BY

REAR ADMIRAL GEORGE J. DUFEK

COMMANDER, U.S. NAVAL SUPPORT FORCE ANTARCTICA AND AUTHOR OF "OPERATION DEEPFREEZE"

"Give wind and tide a chance to change."
—RICHARD E. BYRD

I LEARNED TO handle a ship in polar ice on Rear Admiral Richard E. Byrd's Antarctic expedition of 1939–40. I was a lieutenant and navigator on his flagship.

Admiral Byrd wanted to penetrate the ice of Sulzberger Bay farther than any other vessel had been able to go before. But the small wooden ship, *U.S.S. Bear,* became locked in the ice.

Her sails were useless. Her low-powered engine with its 600-horsepower auxiliary Diesel could not break her free.

"Patience, that's what you need in the Antarctic," Admiral Byrd said as he paced the bridge around the tiny pilothouse. "Wait—give wind and tide a chance to change. It will loosen the ice and allow us to go on."

Turning to me, the Admiral said, "Remember that, George. It applies to life, too. When you get stuck, don't give up. Be patient. Wait. Hold what you have. Circumstances will change and let you go on again."

We got through the ice in Sulzberger Bay, and in the years since then I have found the Admiral's philosophy to be true. On two expeditions to the Arctic and three more to the Antarctic, I learned the value of patience.

Men grow restless and bored when nature's stubbornness makes them wait for favorable conditions. I have read hundreds of books waiting for skies to clear and ice to break, and during one long, fierce storm I began to write about my experiences in this frozen frontier.

Recently, during Operation Deepfreeze, the American expedition in support of the International Geophysical Year, I needed patience most when a plane with seven of our men was lost. There have been so many times in my life, like those days, when all the experience and resources at my command have been futile. I could not control the weather, or the winds, or the ice.

I believe men should work hard when there is something they can do, but when there is nothing left to do, patience is better than pessimism. At these times, I would go to my cabin and pray.

It has always worked. The skies and weather would clear, we would get a rescue plane into the air, and our lost comrades would be found.

I can't explain it and I don't intend to try.

Understanding

BY

DONALD CULROSS PEATTIE

AUTHOR AND NATURALIST

"We are all ignorant. We are just ignorant about different things."

—WILL ROGERS

HERE ARE WORDS to make a man smile—then bow his head a moment, and finally stand all the straighter. For they give him courage, even as they make him humble.

They tell us how much we need one another. They show us how each of us has his place and his job to do. They level us all down, and then lift us all up, in eagerness, in hope to learn a little about the lot we don't know. Said with the easy kindness of a man at once simple and wise, they are a directive toward democracy.

The pride of the intellectual is a Lucifer danger, which in

the recent past has led fine minds as far as the betrayal of their country. The know-how of the expert can be, without wider vision, no more than a blind alley. The fixed idea of the opinionated is as dangerous as a blunt instrument. And the complacency of the incurious is a kind of death in life.

But to know how little you know, and to turn—with the friendliness of a Will Rogers—to others to learn from them is worthy of the greatest mind and possible to the least instructed.

We must seek, across all barriers of kind and caste, of country and color, to understand those ignorant of what we know, yet wise in their own ways. Only then will we master the ultimate lesson—how to live together in peace here on earth, our common home.

Discipline

BY

BRUCE CATTON

PULITZER PRIZE HISTORIAN AND AUTHOR OF
"THIS HALLOWED GROUND"

"Teach him to deny himself."
—ROBERT E. LEE

TOWARD THE END of his tragic, devoted life, General Robert E. Lee attended the christening of a friend's child. The mother asked him for words that would guide the child along the long road to manhood.

Lee's answer summed up the creed that had borne him, through struggle and suffering, to a great place in the American legend.

"Teach him," he said simply, "to deny himself."

To deny himself . . . Unexpected words, coming from a great soldier? One wonders how the young mother felt, hearing them. Even more, one wonders how this advice would strike the average parent of today.

We don't emphasize self-denial very much these days, either for our children or for ourselves. Instead we concentrate on our wants. We seem to have the notion that the world owes us all manner of good things, and we feel abused when we don't get them. Self-discipline is a bore; and as a result we are perilously close to winning an unwelcome fame as a land known for its spoiled children and discontented adults.

To learn to get along without, to realize that what the world is going to demand of us may be a good deal more important than what we are entitled to demand of it—this is a hard lesson. We have not been working very hard at it in recent years. Instead we have developed a moral and intellectual flabbiness that could be fatal to us as individuals and as a nation.

For the world itself is really no easier now than it was in General Lee's time. It offers rich opportunities, but above everything else it offers a struggle, a struggle that will never be won by the self-indulgent. More than anything else, we need to relearn General Lee's lesson.

To deny ourselves . . That way we miss a good many of

the nice, easy things that it is so pleasant to have. But we end up serving something bigger than ourselves. We can finish by attaining greatness.

EDITOR'S NOTE: *This selection is one of fifteen contributions by Bruce Catton to* This Week's *"Words to Live By" page. They have been assembled in an anthology,* Words America Lives By, *published by Doubleday & Company, Inc.*

Faith

BY

IRWIN EDMAN

AUTHOR OF "PHILOSOPHER'S QUEST"

"A shipwrecked sailor on this coast bids you set sail. Full many a gallant ship ere we were lost weathered the gale."

—GREEK INSCRIPTION

THE ABOVE VERSE is the translation of an epitaph on the tombstone of a Greek sailor whose body had been washed ashore on the coast of Asia Minor two thousand years ago.

The quotation has haunted me ever since I first came across it. It seems to me it has a peculiar and poignant meaning for our time. We are accustoming ourselves too much to the language of defeat and disillusion. The imminence of a third world war haunts our dreams, our thoughts, and even the conduct of our practical daily affairs. We read and we repeat that the survival of civilization itself is threatened.

Civilization is indeed imperiled, the future of mankind is precarious and life itself a grave uncertainty. But this in itself is nothing new. To live has always been a risk, and every enterprise a gamble and an act of faith. Ideals have ended in failure before now and idealists have died without having succeeded, however high and however generous their goals.

But the epitaph of the shipwrecked sailor reminds us that, in spite of the many dangers, ships do arrive, sailors do accomplish their course.

In a world where the signs of floundering and shipwreck are all about us—ruined cities and a lost peace—it is well to remind ourselves that we can but try again, and hope for success. The very faith in the possibility of victory over ruin and corruption may help us to win victory. The very faith that a peaceful and just world is possible may help to bring it about.

PART TWO

Living With Other People

The Other Fellow by Clifton Fadiman
Look Inside the Husk by Dr. Maxwell Maltz
Friendship Mending by Frank V. Morley
On Frankness by Robert Hillyer
On Love by Erich Fromm
On Hate by Sloan Wilson
On Playing God by Barbara Cary
All Men Are Born Good by Henry H. Curran
Something More by Albert Schweitzer

The Other Fellow

BY

CLIFTON FADIMAN

WRITER AND LECTURER

"The worst sin toward our fellow creatures is not to hate them, but to be indifferent to them: that's the essence of inhumanity."

—GEORGE BERNARD SHAW

ALONE, no man can save himself. Alone, no man can find himself. Alone on his island, Robinson Crusoe was merely a highly ingenious animal. With the arrival of Friday, he became a man.

We cannot love all our fellow men, except in the most abstract way. But we can at least not be indifferent to them. We can cultivate awareness; we can try always to connect. What is civilization, after all? Surely it is man's effort to grow away from his original state of brutal separateness, of indifference.

It is the bridge one man throws up to connect himself with another man.

The sense of connection is like a muscle. Unused, it withers. Exercised, it grows. Look at the next strange face you see, in a train, a theater lobby, behind a counter—but *really* look at it. Behind those eyes there is a whole life, as complicated, as mysterious as your own. If, for only a fleeting instant, you can feel the pressure of that life, you have hailed in passing that unique miracle—the other fellow.

Look Inside the Husk

BY

DR. MAXWELL MALTZ

AUTHOR OF "DOCTOR PYGMALION"

"And what is a weed? A plant whose virtues have not been discovered."

—RALPH WALDO EMERSON

WHEN DID THESE splendid words occur to Emerson? Perhaps one day when the harvest was ready to be gathered home and the bright fields rippled in the wind, wheat for the winter's bread. For, ages ago, wheat was thought to be a weed, quite useless to mankind.

Perhaps on that day, looking at the ripe bronze fields, Emerson was returning from a visit to his friend the teacher Bronson Alcott—that tireless, undefeatable, unquenchable man—and paused to reflect on Alcott's stubborn insistence that it was never the "bad boy" or the dullard who was to blame but those who lacked the patience and the care to probe beneath the surface for what was good, however unpromising or unfriendly that surface might be. There were no "weeds" in Bronson Alcott's schoolroom.

So many times, in clinic and hospital ward, have I seen the apparently hopeless misfit transformed into a hopeful and helpful person—a giver, not a taker—by the simplest display of interest and belief in him. It always makes me wonder how many good citizens, creators and builders and contributors to our common health as a nation, have been lost because someone, somewhere, was misled by the husk and did not see the golden grain within.

I suppose it comes down to this: Our first "must" for every day should be to pause before passing judgment, remembering that the apparently useless weed in the dirt of the roadside may, with care and cultivation, provide tomorrow's bread.

Friendship Mending

BY

FRANK V. MORLEY

AUTHOR AND PUBLISHER

"A man, sir, should keep his friendship in constant repair."

—DR. SAMUEL JOHNSON

THESE WORDS FROM Johnson entered into me as a boy and ever since then have quietly exerted a power of compulsion. I think it was the oddness of the wording which first startled me. Was friendship a thing to be repaired, as if with hammer and nails? Did Johnson mean you should consciously go around, as politicians do, mending fences? I thought I knew what friendship was, and that when it occurred it was just natural, not something to be carpentered.

Yet the simple and puzzling phrase stayed in my mind till suddenly one day the meaning came clear: You can't take friendship for granted. It always needs repair. Cross your two fingers—and even people as close as that can lose touch. They can drift apart. Friendship is something you can't buy and can't command, but you can lose. So it must be refreshed. At all times, and before too late, it needs refreshment.

How, then, does one go about refreshing friendship? "On clean-shirt day," wrote Johnson's biographer, "he went abroad, and paid visits." That was his way. But to my mind the specific details of repairing friendship are not very important. Sound friendships consist of many nameless acts. What matters is the intent—the intent to keep alive something worthy and mutual. This happens when people remember each other, cultivate each other, meet each other a little more than halfway. Such are the ways in which friendship may be shared.

Nothing on earth is more important, for, just as it has been said that "to lose a friend is to die a little," so the reverse is also true, and when you keep a friend you add something to the richness and the worth of life.

On Frankness

BY

ROBERT HILLYER

PULITZER PRIZE POET

"I was angry with my friend: I told my wrath, my wrath did end."

—WILLIAM BLAKE

I HAVE FOUND that these lines in a poem by Blake are well worth remembering. Often they have helped me meet the little but galling irritations which arise because of something that somebody has said or done to me.

It is so easy to misinterpret the words and deeds of others. Conversely, one must be a very tactful person indeed to avoid offending someone else in the course of a busy day. And when such slips occur, it is all too easy for the victim to nurse his pride in silence and cultivate the seeds of enmity with a thousand midnight suspicions.

How can we expect understanding between nations when individuals—friends and kin—are so jumpy?

In my own life, I have found that the answer lies in Blake's couplet. Tell your wrath—but not wrathfully. Find out what is wrong.

Often it turns out that there is some very simple answer. Perhaps I misunderstood my friend entirely. Or perhaps I had unconsciously hoarded up several small resentments of which this one became the climax. Or possibly my friend, nervous and irritable himself, had a momentary impulse to annoy me, which by now he regrets. Whatever the cause, "talking it out" generally made the trouble disappear.

The next two lines in Blake's poem tell what happens if you follow the opposite course:

I was angry with my foe:
I told it not, my wrath did grow.

So unless you really wish to nurse your wrath, letting your good friend become your bitter enemy—and that is a very grave decision—you had better let him know, at once, exactly what is on your mind.

Tell your wrath. Just three words. But, believe me, they are words to live by.

On Love

BY

ERICH FROMM

AUTHOR OF "THE ART OF LOVING"

"There is only one kind of love, but there are a thousand imitations."

—DUC DE LA ROCHEFOUCAULD

THE DEEPEST NEED of man is the need to overcome his separateness, to leave the prison of his aloneness. The full answer to the problem of existence lies in true and mature love.

What is mature love? It is union under the condition of preserving one's integrity, one's individuality. Love is an active power in man, a power which breaks through the walls which separate man from his fellow men, which unites him with others. Love makes him overcome the sense of isolation and separateness, yet it permits him to be himself. In love the paradox occurs that two beings become one and yet remain two.

On Hate

BY

SLOAN WILSON

AUTHOR OF
"THE MAN IN THE GRAY FLANNEL SUIT"

"I shall allow no man to belittle my soul by making me hate him."

—BOOKER T. WASHINGTON

A LONG WHILE AGO I had a job I didn't like and a boss who seemed to me to be a major menace. For months I would come home and tell my wife about all the horrible new atrocities he had committed. Writers are, of course, notoriously thin-skinned, and although I wasn't at all sure I could be a writer at the time, I was fully capable of being temperamental.

"I really hate this guy," I often said to my wife, and when

she remonstrated, I added, "He's just a guy who was made to be hated!"

It was right after one of these stormy sessions that I happened to read these words: "I shall allow no man to belittle my soul by making me hate him."

I have never been so strongly affected by one sentence, for in a flash it showed me how small and mean I had become. The fact that the author of the sentence was a Negro who must have suffered unspeakable indignities on his way up from slavery seemed a special reproach to me. What were my troubles in the office compared to the struggles which had given birth to this defiant magnanimity?

At just about this time I began to work harder at my writing during evenings and weekends. When I stopped wasting energy on hatred, I found I had lots more strength for better things.

On Playing God

BY

BARBARA CARY

WRITER AND EDITOR

"'Tis an awkward thing to play with souls,
And matter enough to save one's own."
—ROBERT BROWNING

ROBERT BROWNING, if you remember, wrote these lines about a man who deliberately lured a woman away from his best friend. He did it with most excellent intentions. The woman was light and wanton and inconstant. ". . . I saw him tangled in her toils. A shame, said I, if she adds just him to her nine-and-ninety other spoils." Perhaps it *was* a shame —but the result of the meddling was disastrous.

Disaster is usually the result of meddling with other people's lives. Yet the world is full of well-intentioned meddlers. They range all the way from people who interfere in the personal lives of their friends to fanatics who try to impose their religious beliefs and political faiths on entire nations. Convinced that they are doing good, they force their ideas on others in much the same way that an impatient mother forces cod-liver oil down the throat of her protesting baby.

Unfortunately, "good," unlike cod-liver oil, cannot be administered by force. There are times when all of us find it difficult to accept this fact. When we see our friends making mistakes or our children faltering and mismanaging their lives, we long to step in and set them straight. We forget that none of us knows enough about other human beings—even about our own children—to risk tampering with their lives. We forget, too, that the falterings and mistakes, whether they be those of individuals or of nations, are an essential part of growth. The chances are that when Browning's bereft lover recovered from the loss of his wanton lady, he set out to find her replica. For each man must live through his own mistakes.

Actually, we all know this. If we ignore it at times it is, perhaps, because it seems easier to manage other people's lives than it does to manage our own. All of us are afraid and uncertain and often our problems are so burdensome that it is a relief to turn away from them and try our hand at solving someone else's. It's a relief and it gratifies our egos, but it's neither wise nor brave. Help, encouragement, friendship and love we can give other people to the utmost of our capacities. But, when it comes to playing with souls, surely it's matter enough to save our own.

All Men Are Born Good

BY

HENRY H. CURRAN

JUSTICE OF THE NEW YORK COURT
OF SPECIAL SESSIONS, RETIRED

"All men are born good."
—CONFUCIUS

SOME MEN SEEM so bad they must have been born that way. That is what we are likely to think, every once in a while, about somebody else. I used to think so, but now I know better. I will not give up a man like that. I will not believe that God started any one of us off that way.

All the little children we see around the world—born bad? No, they were born good, some with less intellect, less physique, less power of will than others, but none of them downright bad. The trouble came later, in the home, in the neighborhood, or in some failure of our scratchy civilization.

It took me a little while to find this out. In school, in youth, in early grown-up life, I supposed occasionally that a man who went wrong had always been wrong. Then I became a judge in the criminal courts. There the defendants taught me better, made me sure, as I am today, that all men are born good.

That may seem strange. On the bench, I had before me every kind of criminal, the biggest sinners and the littlest, the killer, the stick-up robber, the man who hit his wife in a tenement house tiff, the gentle girl who had a mania for shoplifting, the old lady who kicked the other old lady's dog, a thousand other kinds of guilt—and I had to sentence many of them, often to jail. It was not a reassuring background for certainty that all men are born good.

And yet I know they are. I had to talk with all these passing strangers, try the doors of their hearts, learn their lives, put myself in their shoes. It is a very hard thing to do.

Can you really know the other fellow's heart, really stand in his shoes? The judge must try.

And now I know, by the trying, by the biology and religion of experience. There is a spark, a God-given spark of good, in each of those defendants.

You who sit up there today in judgment, take your time and search, and you will find it. Try to kindle it into some sort of fire of kindness or courtesy or unselfishness. Often you will fail, more often you will win.

But never give up. For the spark is there. It always was. All men are born good.

Something More

BY

ALBERT SCHWEITZER

DOCTOR, CLERGYMAN AND MEDICAL MISSIONARY

"Thou shalt love the Lord thy God with all thy heart, and with all thy soul, and with all thy mind. This is the first and great commandment. And the second is like unto it, Thou shalt love thy neighbor as thyself."

—MATTHEW 22:37–39

IT IS NOT ENOUGH merely to exist. It's not enough to say, "I'm earning enough to live and to support my family. I do my work well. I'm a good father. I'm a good husband. I'm a good churchgoer."

That's all very well. *But you must do something more.* Seek always to do some good, somewhere. Every man has to seek in his own way to make his own self more noble and to realize his own true worth.

You must give some time to your fellow man. Even if it's a little thing, do something for those who have need of a man's help, something for which you get no pay but the privilege of doing it. For remember, you don't live in a world all your own. *Your brothers are here, too.*

EDITOR'S NOTE: *This selection has been adapted from an interview with Dr. Schweitzer by Bernard S. Redmont published in* This Week *on November 18, 1951.*

PART THREE

Living With The World

Your Magic Moment

BY

MARK VAN DOREN

AUTHOR AND PULITZER PRIZE POET

"Only one person in a thousand knows the trick of really living in the present."

—STORM JAMESON

OF ALL SAD things we tell ourselves, the saddest is: "I didn't make the most of the occasion." We go to say goodbye; an old friend comes to see us; somebody does us a kindness; we have an argument; we meet a new acquaintance; and somehow we don't do justice to the moment.

Afterward we try to imagine that we did; we make believe; we hear ourselves saying all the things we should have said; but then it is too late. And the most we can do in the circumstances is to resolve that the next time . . .

The next time, we say, will be different, but the danger is

just as great that the next time, too, we shall fail.

Men cannot see into the future, and so we shouldn't lament too much our failures to realize what moments mean before they are remembered. But there is one thing we can do, and the happiest people are those who do it to the limit of their ability.

We can be completely present. We can be all there. We can control the tendency of our minds to wander from the situation we are in toward yesterday, toward tomorrow, toward something we have forgotten, toward some other place we are going next. It is hard to do this, but it is harder to understand afterward wherein it was we fell so short. It was where and when we ceased to give our entire attention to the person, the opportunity, before us.

Those who have fewest regrets are those who take each moment as it comes for all that it is worth. It will never come again, for worse or better. It is ours alone, we can make it what we will.

Slow Down

BY

EDDIE CANTOR

COMEDIAN

"A poor life this, if full of care,
We have no time to stand and stare."
—W. H. DAVIES

AS A YOUNG fellow, I was in a hurry to hit the top. Like a horse wearing blinders, I raced ahead seeing nothing but the finish line. My grandmother worried. "Don't go so fast, son," she'd say, "or you'll miss the scenery." I paid no attention. When a man knows where he's going, why waste time getting there?

The years flew by. I had fame, financial security, and a devoted family. Why I wasn't "the most happy fella" was beyond me. I raced on.

A Ziegfeld show in which I starred opened out of town.

When the curtain fell, the applause was long, loud and beautiful. We had a hit. Backstage was charged with excitement. Somebody handed me a telegram. It was from Ida. Our fourth daughter had been born. Another of my children starting life without me. Natalie had been six months old before I even saw her. Suddenly, above the applause still ringing in my ears, I heard my grandmother's voice, "Don't go so fast, son, or you'll miss the scenery."

Oh, how much I had missed! The first faltering steps of my little girls; the tears I hadn't wiped away; the bright sayings, heard only from their mother over a phone.

I thought of friends collected, and then neglected; of my library, full of books with uncut pages; of vacations promised to my wife.

Ever since that "moment of truth," despite a full schedule, I've made it a point to pause now and again to enjoy "the scenery." Those pauses have become more important than any full schedule I ever had, because it's not only the scenery you miss by going too fast—you also miss the sense of where you're going and why.

Beauty

BY

FRANK LLOYD WRIGHT

ARCHITECT

"'Beauty is truth, truth beauty,'—that is all ye know on earth and all ye need to know."

—JOHN KEATS

PEOPLE ARE forever saying, "Oh, that's beautiful but it isn't practical." As an architect more than sixty years, I have learned that only the beautiful is practical. And conversely, anything that is truly practical, functional and useful is beautiful—whether it be a sunset or some man-made object. When we perceive a thing to be beautiful, it is because we instinctively recognize its rightness.

You can apply "the practical is beautiful" or "the beautiful is practical" principle to your everyday life, whether you live in a castle or a hut. The beautiful is not ornate or needlessly expensive. On the contrary, excess is always vulgar.

But you must first learn to recognize the beautiful, have the disposition to cherish it and the intelligence to distinguish it from what is merely curious. When we lack the knowledge of the difference, we find ugliness—never beauty. Today, unfortunately, many human beings, like bushels of grain, are poured out and trampled in our cities. But the eventual City of the Future will contain all of the practical products of industry and yet have beauty for every inhabitant.

In everyday life, you can be guided by beauty in whatever you undertake—whether making a dress or a bookcase. To achieve the superior, you must first refuse to accept the inferior. Look for the light and you won't dwell in darkness. You will then bring out something in yourself which is both practical and beautiful.

The longer I live the more beautiful life becomes. The earth's beauty grows on me. If you foolishly ignore beauty, you'll soon find yourself without it. Your life will be impoverished. But if you wisely invest in beauty, it will remain with you all the days of your life.

The Land Around Us

BY

RACHEL L. CARSON

AUTHOR OF "THE SEA AROUND US"

"The exceeding beauty of the earth, in her splendor of life, yields a new thought with every petal. The hours when the mind is absorbed by beauty are the only hours when we really live, so that the longer we can stay among these things so much the more is snatched from inevitable Time."
—RICHARD JEFFERIES, *The Pageant of Summer.*

IT WAS ABOUT a decade ago that I first discovered in the writings of Jefferies these lines that so impressed themselves upon my mind. They are, in a way, a statement of a creed I have always lived by, for a preoccupation with the wonder and beauty of the earth has strongly influenced the course of my life.

It is a preoccupation that has yielded a rich store of memories—mental pictures of wild swans adrift on a mountain lake, repeating in their plumage the snowy white of the peaks beyond; of salmon leaping in the frothy water of a mountain stream high in the dripping forests of the Cascades; of the veery's song in the green dusk of a wooded valley.

In the darker hours of life I have often drawn upon such memories for deep and never failing comfort, or I have gone out to replenish my store and find again the refreshment of the natural world. For in the words of Keats, "Some shape of beauty moves away the pall from our dark spirits."

In recent months it has been my privilege to receive many letters from people who, like myself, have been steadied and reassured by contemplating the long history of earth and sea and the deeper meanings of the world of nature.

There is symbolic as well as actual beauty in the migration of the birds; in the ebb and flow of the tides, responding to sun and moon as they have done for untold millions of years; in the repose of the folded bud in winter, ready within its sheath for the spring. There is something infinitely healing in these repeated refrains of nature, the assurance that after night, dawn comes, and spring after the winter.

It is a wholesome and necessary thing for us to turn again to the earth and in the contemplation of her beauties to know the sense of wonder and humility. There is modern truth in the ancient wisdom of the psalmist: "I will lift up mine eyes unto the hills, from whence cometh my help."

The Sky Above Us

BY

DAVID McCORD

POET AND ESSAYIST

"The sky is the daily bread of the eyes."
—RALPH WALDO EMERSON

ONE WORLD is a phrase of our own time, but man has always had One Roof. The sky is the same everywhere. It is different only in the kind and quality of its clouds. And there was never an uninteresting cloud. "Very like a whale," said Polonius, speaking of one. Very like a thousand things, but never just like another cloud.

All day, rain or shine, the world over, the pageant of the sky is somewhere visible. And all night, if there is a moon. It is, by a paradox, the greatest show on earth. It is also the most universal, for it visibly provides the enormous backdrop in our spiritual drama. The show is never repeated exactly the same way twice, and it costs nothing to see.

The sky is what the prisoner longs for and what the city dweller often forgets. Walk down a western avenue of any town in the face of a brilliant sunset, and who has stopped in his tracks to see it better? Who has lifted his head? Not many; very few. And what person at a window at home, in a train, on a ship, or in a stratocruiser lays down his murder story or interrupts a casual conversation to look for a moment in reverence at the sky? Almost no one.

Yet it is the immensity of the sky which can turn happiness to exaltation, comfort us in grief and offer to those who long for something the bright intimation of hope or escape. It is the oldest symbol of freedom known to man.

For my part, I know the sky better than my city or my state. Wherever I am, the night is full of familiar stars, and every day—unless rain or snow or illness has interfered—there is at least one crowded moment of renewed adventure through the cumulus mountains, down the black canyons of storm, across the mackerel Sahara, up the cirro-vapor trails or under the drifting cotton of a summer afternoon.

How often have you looked at it today? Did the sun's rays move like a giant compass through the crack in the western wall? What shapes did you see? Did you spot a camel, a shark, an Everest, a face, a dragon, or a castle door?

Emerson was right. The sky is the daily bread of the eyes—and of the mind, and the imagination too. So whenever the world appears to be at its worst, take a look at the wayward splendor overhead. The chances are it will be at its best.

The Little Things

BY

EDWIN WAY TEALE

AUTHOR OF "INSECT LIFE,"
"CIRCLE OF THE SEASONS"

"Let us dig our furrow in the fields of the commonplace."

—J. HENRI FABRE

THE HAPPIEST MEN I have known have been those who found their pleasures in simple things. Like J. Henri Fabre, the peasant-born student of the insects who spent most of his long life exploring a pebbly, thistly acre or two in the south of France, they have sought their adventures near at home.

Another case is that of a gentle naturalist who for more than eighty years lived on Staten Island and was familiar with all the back roads, knew the hidden whereabouts of the rarest wildflowers, noted the arrival and departure of the birds.

When he died in 1945, William T. David had become world-famous as America's leading authority on the cicadas. Yet all his life he lived within two hundred feet of the spot where he was born.

I often wonder if any of the roaming men who sailed away, past Staten Island, out of New York Harbor, to far ends of the earth ever found as much of interest, or of happiness, during those eight decades, as my friend discovered close to his own door.

The greenness of the grass beyond the fence is proverbial. The Happy Valley seems always to lie over another ridge. An ever recurring fallacy is the belief that we have only to move to leave our troubles behind, that somewhere else we will be different and life will be interesting. But, as the wisdom of the East has it: "*They change their skies but not themselves who cross the seven seas.*"

Only a mile or so from his birthplace in Concord, Massachusetts, Henry Thoreau had the great adventure of his life in his hut behind Walden Pond. He spoke the literal truth when he said he had "traveled a good deal in Concord." Traveling widely at home lies within reach of us all. And, in truth, if we find nothing of lasting interest where we are, we are likely to find little of lasting interest where we wish to go.

How to Meet a Very Nice Person

BY

HENRY KING

MOVIE PRODUCER AND DIRECTOR

"We must relearn to be alone."
—ANNE MORROW LINDBERGH, *Gift from the Sea*

IN TODAY'S crowded civilization and in this busy and active society, man is finding it increasingly difficult to indulge one of the most priceless luxuries which life can give: occasional total solitude.

Being alone does not mean being lonely. It means cutting off the external, the superficial and the superfluous, and seeking instead the inner strength which one finds best in solitude. It enriches the spirit and ennobles the man, and one who denies himself its refuge is not living life to its fullest.

Saints and geniuses have found their greatest inspiration in solitude. It can bring rewards to all of us.

You don't have to be a rebel or an eccentric in order to spend some time alone. A walk alone at dusk, an early hour of solitude watching the dawn break, an idle interval on a garden bench, a short, slow drive on back roads in beautiful country—no life is too busy for moments like these.

I happen to be a member of the Civil Air Patrol and spend a certain amount of time alone at the controls of my plane. I find these hours refreshing and productive. In the limitless reaches of the sky a man is really alone. The problems which seemed so difficult to master in the turmoil of the office and the studio resolve themselves when one is alone.

Everything pulls itself back into perspective, often a better perspective. One gets a chance to stop and analyze one's worries—and dismiss them! The armor which all of us assume in our social contacts falls away. We are at peace with ourselves again.

Don't be afraid of being alone now and then. If you are—watch out. Something is wrong.

Make it a point to stop and take time to make your own acquaintance. You'll probably get something of a surprise. Because you'll be meeting a very nice and stimulating person—yourself!

Remember Now

BY

ALEC WAUGH

"We never do anything, consciously, for the last time, without sadness of heart."

—THOMAS DE QUINCEY

I WAS SEVENTEEN when I first read that sentence by De Quincey. I was in an Army training camp. I loathed it there, everything about it—the impersonal military machine, the monotonous routine of drills and musketry, the arrogance of the officers, the officiousness of the N.C.O.s. I laughed when I read that sentence. It would not be true of *me* when I left this place!

Yet when my turn came to shoulder my kitbag to the station, I found myself remembering my occasional good times there and the friends with whom I had grumbled through the many bad ones. I felt nostalgic, and as the train drew out I craned my neck to catch a last look of the parade ground. After all, De Quincey was proved right.

I have never forgotten the lesson I learned that morning. As a travel writer and a soldier—I have spent ten years in khaki—I have frequently found myself in uncongenial atmospheres. I have many times counted the hours to the sailing of a ship and the arrival of a posting order. At such periods those thirteen words have been a genuine help and consolation. However despondent I may have felt, I have reminded myself that when the time came to go I should feel sad, which meant that what I was doing at the time was not too bad after all.

That knowledge has made it easier for me to live in and for the moment, to appreciate an immediate pleasure without looking four hours back or five hours ahead. In particular it has helped me to develop the possibilities and potentialities of each chance friendship, and nothing is intolerable that can be shared. Thanks to De Quincey, at even the dreariest times I have been able to think each morning when I awake, "Something is almost certain to happen today that I'll enjoy."

The Test

BY

NANCY WILSON ROSS

AUTHOR OF "THE RETURN OF LADY BRACE" AND "THE LEFT HAND IS THE DREAMER"

> *"Can you walk on water? You have done no better than a straw. Can you fly in the air? You have done no better than a bluebottle. Conquer your heart; then you may become somebody."*
>
> —ANSARI OF HERAT

NOT LONG AGO, when the front pages were filled with rockets and space ships, missiles and artificial moons, I was turning the pages of Aldous Huxley's *The Perennial Philosophy* and came upon the lines above, from Ansari of Herat, who was a Persian philosopher of the eleventh century.

I have not forgotten, and probably never will, the impact of those simple sentences in the late silence of a winter night.

Over and over again in this age of satellites those words from nine hundred years ago come back to me. They seem of special significance at just this time in history.

No matter if man should be able at last to establish a bridgehead on the pitted surface of the moon. Or if he should find possible living conditions beneath the lowering clouds of the planet Venus. Or even if he perfects a rocket that would take a band of space pioneers—prepared to produce children and grandchildren en route—far beyond our Earth into another solar system. These intrepid voyagers into space would still carry with them the very same human equipment as those they left behind.

So, when man conquers space, his ancient, universal and perpetual problem will remain the same—as it has been from the very beginning—*to conquer himself.*

PART FOUR

"It Goes On!"

I BELIEVE BY John Peck
THE AWAKENING BY Boris Pasternak
ON FAITH BY J. Edgar Hoover
ON MEDITATION BY Howard Van Smith
ROBERT FROST'S SECRET BY Ray Josephs
GOD'S HELP BY Margaret Mead
ON LIVING FOREVER BY General Lucius D. Clay
ON YOUTH BY the Reverend Robert I. Gannon, S.J.
THE CLUE BY Mildred Cram
ON PRAYER BY Dr. Edward A. Strecker
SOME PRAYERS
A FAMILY PRAYER
A MORNING PRAYER
A THANKFUL PRAYER
A PRACTICAL PRAYER
THE PERFECT PRAYER
A GOOD RESOLVE

I Believe

BY

JOHN PECK

BRITISH FOREIGN SERVICE OFFICER

"I believe . . ."
—THE APOSTLES' CREED

TO ME, these two tremendous words proclaim what lies at the heart of the mystery of man and the universe. And much of today's doubt and perplexity stems from the fact that their significance is forgotten.

The Creed does not say, "It is believed that . . ." or "There is a general belief that . . . ," but *"I believe."* For there is nothing in the world that can believe, or know, or deny, or choose, except the individual human being.

No talk of governments deciding, or committees recommending, or the people electing, can suppress the fact that any group is a collection of individuals, each making his own personal decision. There is no act of nations, groups of nations, or groups within the state which is not ultimately an individual personal responsibility.

"I believe" is harder to say than "I don't know," much harder than "I don't care." For the scientist seeking knowledge and proof, it is very hard indeed, unless he admits that the impulse driving him to discovery is something beyond final proof.

And now when we stand upon the edge of space it is supremely important for every individual not only to consider what he believes, but also to reflect, simply, that he *can* believe. This is the foundation of humility and wisdom, and of our hope for the future.

The Awakening

BY

BORIS PASTERNAK

FAMOUS SOVIET WRITER, AUTHOR OF
"DOCTOR ZHIVAGO"

"The wise man looks inside his heart and finds eternal peace."

—HINDU PROVERB

IN THIS ERA of world wars, in this atomic age, the values have changed. We have learned that we are the guests of existence, travelers between two stations. We must discover security within ourselves.

During our short span of life we must find our own insights into our relationship with the existence in which we participate so briefly. Otherwise, we cannot live. This means, as I see it, a departure from the materialistic view of the nineteenth century. It means a reawakening of the spiritual world, of our inner life—of religion. I don't mean religion as a dogma or as a church, but as a vital feeling.

EDITOR'S NOTE: *This selection has been adapted from an interview with Boris Pasternak by Nils Ake Nilsson, director of the Russian Institute at the University of Stockholm, which first appeared in* The Reporter *magazine on November 27, 1958.*

On Faith

BY

J. EDGAR HOOVER

DIRECTOR OF THE F.B.I.

"Trust in the Lord with all thine heart, and lean not unto thine own understanding."

—PROVERBS 3:5

THROUGH MANY YEARS of active life, and the observation of many kinds of people, I have found that the strongest, wisest, most competent and reliable man is also the first to admit his inadequacy.

Contradictory though it may sound, he is strong because he is humble—and remembers always that man is the creation of God. No rule of life is more basic.

When man "leans on his own understanding," when he lives by his own strength, when he boasts of probing the mysteries of the atom, the depths of the sea or the secrets of outer space, he forgets God and claims he is his own master. The result is untold suffering.

Even though one's position is maintained, even though material wealth increases, success quickly turns to failure when God has been forgotten. There is no peace of mind, no personal satisfaction, no personal experience of inward joy.

To "trust in the Lord with all thine heart" is a mark of strength. And it is the only path to happiness, success and true fulfillment.

On Meditation

BY

HOWARD VAN SMITH

NEWSPAPERMAN

"To be alone with Silence is to be alone with God."
—SAMUEL MILLER HAGEMAN

A FRIEND of mine, a man in his late fifties, has such a benign calmness about him that just being with him brings a feeling of peace. One day I asked him how in a world of rushed and harried people he maintained such evenness of disposition.

"I've been asked that before," he said, "and I believe I confused my questioner. My answer was 'Silence.' I find it's the greatest refresher there is."

I wasn't surprised, for I hadn't expected an ordinary answer. But how could anyone put silence to work?

"You simply enjoy it," he said with a smile. "Usually the senses are bringing so much sight, sound and other things to us that they occupy most of our time. But to sit in silence now and then, with the outside world withheld, means to cut all this off and free the mind so that it can become itself."

"You mean all you do is just sit still and think."

"No, not exactly," he said. "You see, thinking, using words, is an echo of sound. I mean detaching the mind from all outside activity so that, in a sense, there is nothing there but itself."

I smiled too but I feared he had carried me along now beyond my depth.

"What comes to you when you do this?" I asked.

"Why, peace, repose. There's a great deal of power in this kind of silence. But I wouldn't try to describe it. The only answer is for you to try it yourself."

Since then I have followed his advice. It wasn't so easy at first, detaching the mind from all the outside activity that usually controls it, but I wouldn't trade this practice now for anything in the world. I've been surprised too to learn how many others do it. Some businessmen close the doors of their offices for five minutes at a certain time each day. They say there comes a calming away of the daily strain which nothing else can bring.

What is this wonderful power of silence?

I agree with my friend when he said he would not try to

describe it. But one important result is a conserving of the bodily and mental forces we so easily waste. And sometimes too I think you gain a new sense of being, you learn to know that still part of you that lies behind all life's activities, that quiet consciousness that is forever yourself.

But, as my friend said, the only way to know the peace this brings is to try it yourself.

Robert Frost's Secret

BY

RAY JOSEPHS

JOURNALIST AND AUTHOR

"It goes on . . ."
—ROBERT FROST

IT WAS my good luck to be present at the eightieth birthday celebration in honor of Robert Frost, America's most distinguished living poet, four-time Pulitzer Prize winner. All day long he had been answering questions, but one question had not been put.

"In all your years and all your travels," I asked, "what do you think is the most important thing you've learned about life?"

He paused a moment, then with the twinkle sparkling under those brambly eyebrows he replied:

"In three words, I can sum up everything I've learned about life: *It goes on.* In all the confusions of today, with all our troubles, with politicians and people slinging the word 'fear' around, all of us become discouraged, tempted to say this is the end, the finish. But life—it goes on. It always has. It always will. Don't forget that.

"Just a little while back, at my farm near Ripton, Vermont, I planted a few more trees. You wonder why? Well, I'm like the Chinese of ninety who did the same thing. When they asked him why, he said that the world wasn't a desert when he came into it and wouldn't be when he departed. Those trees will keep on growing after I'm gone and after you're gone.

"I don't hold with people who say, 'Where do we go from here?' or 'What's the use?' I wouldn't get up in the morning if I thought we didn't have a direction to go in. But if you ask me what the direction is, I can't answer. It's different for each of us. The important thing to remember is that there is a direction and a continuity even if so often we think we're lost.

"Despite our fears and worries—and they're very real to all of us—life continues . . . it goes on. Three words above all else. In my eighty years, that I've learned."

God's Help

BY

MARGARET MEAD

AUTHOR AND ANTHROPOLOGIST

"Get the distaff ready, and God will send the flax."
—MY GRANDMOTHER

THESE WERE WORDS my grandmother used to say. She said them, not as a promise or an admonition, but as a simple statement of fact about the way the world worked. I used to spend a lot of time thinking what it meant. The distaff was a man-made tool, shaped for a special purpose, that of making thread. It was intended for no other use. So the proverb, I decided, meant that we must "meet God halfway," doing our best to help ourselves. But also, it meant we have to be specifically ready for opportunity, not just virtuously sitting around waiting for a call from heaven. We have to know exactly what we mean to do, and be fully prepared to do it—with God's help.

It's good to make plans, to dream of a distant goal, but only if the dreaming is accompanied by realistic effort on our part. When I was a child, this idea seemed a simple way of saying that life was to be trusted, like the motto that hung in the office of a country doctor whom I loved: "All things work together for good to them that love God." Later it came to mean something else to me too, something very special about the strength of American character, which has this very combination of trust and enterprising effort.

We cannot bind the future by making rigid plans and stubbornly sticking to them. But we can instead get the distaff ready for the thread which is not yet spun and for which there is as yet no flax.

On Living Forever

BY

GENERAL LUCIUS D. CLAY

FORMER U.S. MILITARY GOVERNOR IN GERMANY

"If a man leaves children behind him, it is as if he did not die."

—MOROCCAN PROVERB

NO ONE EVER achieves all his hopes and aspirations. No one is ever sure, in looking back, that he has played his full part in making a better world. But as we live again in our children and our children's children, we do not need to be afraid. For we can touch the future with our children's hands. We can look to them to correct our failures, to achieve many of our hopes and aspirations which never came true for us.

Today we live in a temporarily troubled world and our

generation must continue to do its utmost to restore order and stability. But even if we do not succeed in full, we may still face the future with optimism and with certain knowledge that our children can bring into being many of the things which we have just begun. Perhaps they may make it possible for their children to live in a world of peace and understanding.

Much is being said of the present crisis in world affairs and the need to do something about it. But to play a part and do our duty, we do not need to be the principal actors. We have only to be good citizens, good neighbors and—most of all—good parents.

On Youth

BY

THE REVEREND ROBERT I.
GANNON, S.J.

FORMER PRESIDENT, FORDHAM UNIVERSITY

"History teaches us to hope."
—ROBERT E. LEE

THE GROWING LAXITY of personal morals has always startled everyone over fifty. The increasing confusion in education, the chaotic changes which are coming over the governments of the world, have alarmed every thinking man in a dozen different generations.

If you read your Spengler or Huizinga and take them seriously, you will want to give up now; you will want to climb into the ark, shut the door and ride the flood. But that is because you belong to a mature generation. You have been battered by years; you are conscious of difficulties, wearied by problems, and depressed by the logic which tells you that if things go on as they are, civilization will fly apart.

Fortunately, however, there is always an element in the world too young to worry. There is always a buoyant surge of life coming up from below, strong, confident, happy—and ignorant. But part of youth's ignorance is a blessing in disguise; for the difficulties and complexities which we older ones have watched accumulating over the years present, for them, a normal problem. This they proceed to attack with forces we no longer possess and, as a result, somehow the world keeps turning.

And to help them, there is always in the background "a divinity that shapes our ends," an all-wise, all-holy and all-powerful God, Who has a very mysterious and wonderful way of bringing good out of evil.

The Clue

BY

MILDRED CRAM

AUTHOR OF "FOREVER" AND "THE PROMISE"

"Our Creator would never have made such lovely days and have given us the deep hearts to enjoy them, above and beyond all thought, unless we were meant to be immortal."

—NATHANIEL HAWTHORNE

THE PROOF of immortality is all around us. We see it in the sunset, flakes of salmon, rose and gold; and in the stars, scattered like crystal dust across the night sky. Or in the shadow of a flock of geese dimming the moon.

We see it in the dawn. The stir and rustle of the waking earth as the globe turns toward the sun. A cock crow, challenging, full of hope.

There is proof of immortality in such miracles as the thrust of Indian pipe through sodden pine needles . . . the flash of trout in a deep pool . . . tugging tides and salt marshes . . . wind in grain.

Given the deep heart to recognize and to enjoy such things, man need never question life everlasting.

On Prayer

BY

DR. EDWARD A. STRECKER

PSYCHIATRIST AND AUTHOR

"Hold prayer in high esteem. It is the foundation of all the virtues, and the source of all grace needed to sanctify ourselves and to discharge the duties of our employment."
—Adapted from ST. JEAN BAPTISTE DE LA SALLE

PRAYER IS THE LANGUAGE of religion; but it is also a mighty force in our daily life. That is the wisdom expressed in these words by La Salle, the priestly educator, whose three hundredth anniversary was celebrated a few years ago.

A doctor sees many examples of the power of prayer. Obviously, there is small value to the mere hasty mumbling of a formula of words. Nor should prayer be the medium of barter with God—"If You do this for me, I will do that for You." Such prayer is reminiscent of the pack rat, which takes something valuable, perhaps jewelry, leaving in exchange a scrap of paper or a pebble. But true prayer—by which I mean sincerely lifting your mind and heart to God—can change your life.

For example, prayer has an important place in psychiatric treatment. Often the psychiatrist finds it necessary to help the patient relinquish excessive and childish emotional dependencies upon others. Through prayer, the patient can take his troubles to God and find the support and strength he needs.

Only a few years ago the eminent psychoanalyst Jung wrote: "In thirty years I have treated many patients. Among all my patients in the second half of life, every one of them fell ill because he had lost that which the living religions of every age had given their followers, and none of them was really healed who did not regain his religious outlook."

Here is evidence that La Salle's words are as true today as when he spoke them long ago as founder of the Christian Brothers, who today conduct schools and colleges throughout the world. Now, as always, for the sake of our work in life, we must "hold prayer in high esteem."

Some Prayers

Editor's Note: *In addition to the customary "Words to Live By" selections, prayers have often appeared on* This Week's *opening page. Here are a few of those which readers tell us have been most helpful.*

A Family Prayer

LORD, BEHOLD our family here assembled. We thank Thee for this place in which we dwell; for the love that unites us; for the peace accorded us this day; for the hope with which we expect the morrow; for the health, the work, the food and the bright skies that make our lives delightful; for our friends in all parts of the earth, and our friendly helpers in this foreign isle.

Let peace abound in our small company. Purge out of every heart the lurking grudge. Give us grace and strength to forbear and persevere. Offenders, give us the grace to accept and to forgive offenders. Forgetful ourselves, help us to bear cheerfully the forgetfulness of others.

Give us courage, gaiety and the quiet mind. Spare to us

our friends, soften to us our enemies. Bless us, if it may be, in all our innocent endeavors. If it may not, give us the strength to encounter that which is to come, that we be brave in peril, constant in tribulation, temperate in wrath, and in all changes of fortune and down to the gates of death, loyal and loving one to another.

As the clay to the potter, as the windmill to the wind, as children of their sire, we beseech of Thee this help and mercy for Christ's sake. Amen.

—ROBERT LOUIS STEVENSON

(*This prayer was written while Stevenson, gravely ill with tuberculosis, was a voluntary exile in Samoa.*)

A Morning Prayer

THIS IS the day which the Lord hath made: let us be glad and rejoice therein.

—PSALMS 117

A Thankful Prayer

O GOD, Thou hast given so much to us, give one thing more—a grateful heart. Amen.

—GEORGE HERBERT

A Practical Prayer

O GOD, give us serenity to accept what cannot be changed; courage to change what should be changed; and wisdom to distinguish the one from the other.

EDITOR'S NOTE: *This prayer is often regarded as a piece of wisdom generations old whose author is unknown. Actually, it was written by Dr. Reinhold Niebuhr, for many years professor of Applied Christianity at the Union Theological Seminary in New York City, and first published in 1935 as part of a pamphlet by Howard Chandler Robbins. Its message was so persuasive that it was copied many times, often without credit to Dr. Niebuhr, and thus gradually the mantle of age descended upon the words, as indicated in the story told by I. A. R. Wylie on page 100. She had come to know the words as a "centuries-old prayer," and believed them to have been written by a soldier.*

The Perfect Prayer

LORD, MAKE ME an instrument of Thy Peace. Where there is hatred, let me sow love. Where there is injury, pardon. Where there is doubt, faith. Where there is despair, hope. Where there is darkness, light. Where there is sadness, joy.

O Divine Master, grant that I may not so much seek to be consoled as to console; to be understood as to understand; to be loved, as to love; for it is in giving that we receive, it is in pardoning that we are pardoned, and it is in dying that we are born to Eternal Life.

—ST. FRANCIS OF ASSISI

A Good Resolve

I SHALL be true—for there are those that trust me.

—CHINESE

PART FIVE

"When I Was A Child"

All wisdom does not come from famous philosophers. It grows within families, too. Here are recounted some examples:

How Not to Be Bored

BY

EMILY KIMBROUGH

NOTED TRAVELER, LECTURER, WRITER

"I have never met anyone who couldn't tell me something I hadn't known before."

—MY GRANDFATHER

GRANDFATHER KIMBROUGH took me on a train from Muncie, Indiana, where we lived, to Indianapolis, where we could see a bridge he was building. I was nine years old and I had been Grandfather's companion on many such trips about the state. At that time I was anticipating this particular one because it was to include lunch in a big dining room at the Claypool Hotel, and the grand finale before train time of a chocolate soda at Craig's—a double one. I remember these things only because I have never forgotten Grandfather's conversation with the train conductor.

We had arrived in Indianapolis, the end of the line. Everyone got off the train except Grandfather. He stood on the steps of the parlor car, talking to the conductor. I tugged at his coat; he was so absorbed he paid no attention.

When the conversation ended he took my hand and said, as we walked along the platform, "That was a very interesting thing he told me."

I was cross. The shimmering day ahead—a bridge, a hotel lunch and a chocolate soda—was a long time getting under way. I quickened my step, tugging at Grandfather's hand. I said over my shoulder, "What could a conductor tell you that you didn't know already?" I was not relegating a conductor to a low stratum; I only considered it preposterous that anyone in the world knew more than my companion and idol.

Grandfather stopped so suddenly I was jerked back and around so that I faced him. He wasn't angry—he was arrested by an idea. He looked down at me a long time in such a way that I was held quiet and silent.

"Why, Emily," he said, shaking his head a little in astonishment at his own discovery, "I believe I have never met anyone who couldn't tell me something I hadn't known before."

And that is how it has been for me from that day to this.

Walk Your Own Path

BY

CAMERON HAWLEY

AUTHOR OF "EXECUTIVE SUITE" AND "CASH MCCALL"

"A man finds happiness only by walking his own path."

—MY GRANDMOTHER

ON ONE of the last days of my grandmother's life I sat beside her bed. Warmly reminiscent, she talked of how the world had changed during the half century since she had come to the Dakota Territory in 1878 as a pioneering bride. I asked what change she considered most significant.

Her face sobered. "I'll tell you the one I most regret," she said. "When I was a girl, there were so many men who stood out as individuals. Now there are so few.

"More and more all the time, it seems, men are yielding to some terrible compulsion to conform, to think alike and talk alike—yes, even to look alike. In those days you could recognize any man who was worth knowing as far away as you could see him or hear the sound of his voice. Believe me, no one ever mistook your grandfather for someone else. He was always his own man, thinking with his own mind, standing on his own feet. He knew that a man finds happiness only by walking his own path across the earth."

The intensity of her voice made her words an obviously purposeful warning, but years passed before I appreciated the full value of the heritage she was handing me.

Now, at fifty, looking back over my own life and the work I have done to date, I see so clearly that the things of which I am least proud have resulted from the weakness of conformity, from being more concerned with pleasing others than with satisfying myself.

My successes have come when I have had the sustained courage to follow my grandmother's admonition—in her words, to walk my own path across the earth.

I Say What I Think

BY

LILLI PALMER

STAGE AND SCREEN STAR

"Everybody's friend is everybody's fool."
—MY MOTHER

MY MOTHER was born on the river Rhine, where people are gay and easygoing, where they drink much wine and don't care who likes them. When I was a child I often heard from her a healthy warning, especially when I came crying that someone didn't like me and demanding to know what I could do to make him or her like me.

"Everybody's friend is everybody's fool," she would say serenely; or sometimes, "Many enemies mean much honor," or "Where there's much sun there's much shadow."

I have interpreted those ideas in my own way. I don't set

out to antagonize people, or to be aggressive or provocative, but I have never made a special concession just for the purpose of being liked. I've spoken my mind even when I knew that what I said might be unpopular, because I believe that to speak your mind is essential, to take part in a controversy is important. It has never been my nature to sit back and keep quiet for fear of treading on somebody's toes.

The danger of being too sensitive to what others think is strongly illustrated in the play *Death of a Salesman.* The author makes an important cause of the demoralization of his hero the fact that he cared too much whether he was well liked. He was afraid ever to make an enemy, and this hastened his destruction.

My mother made me immune to that fear in early youth. You can't go through life only making friends, I realized very soon.

If, for a good cause, you must make an enemy, accept the fact. As long as your conscience is clear, you will find that you have strengthened not only your determination but your character.

Reach Up

BY

ALEC WAUGH

ENGLISH NOVELIST AND TRAVELER

"High failure towering o'er low success."
—MY FATHER

OVER SIXTY YEARS ago my father wrote this line in a prize-winning poem at Oxford. These words have meant as much to me as any line I've ever read. For they are a constant reminder that failure on a classic scale is an even keener spur than the immediate rewards of routine success.

Out of his few words come many images: the Spartans dying at Thermopylae . . . brave men vainly trying to scale Mt. Everest . . . Woodrow Wilson fighting for one world at Versailles . . . the glorious evacuation of Dunkirk . . . Bataan.

These are classic examples of men struggling to draw upon reserves they lacked, and they are a nobler tribute to the dignity of the human race, a keener incentive to high endeavor, than the laurels of a Roman triumph. The squares of Europe are littered with the statues of generals, admirals and statesmen whose titles and deeds we have forgotten. But still alive in memory are the men and women who attempted more than they could carry out and left unfinished work that their successors completed.

Too often we are tempted by the effortless and easy thing. At such moments raise your sights, think big, attempt something difficult even if you do not quite bring it off.

"High failure towering o'er low success." Those six words, at moments of hesitation, have rung through my heart and memory—a warning, an inspiration and a challenge.

Birth of an Author

I

BY

WILLIAM SAROYAN

AUTHOR OF "THE TIME OF YOUR LIFE,"
"THE HUMAN COMEDY," ETC.

"It is not impossible to walk on water."
—GARABED SAROYAN

THESE WORDS were said to me about twenty-five years ago by my great-uncle Garabed Saroyan when he came into my bed-living-and-work room in a house in Fresno, California, where I had recently installed a typewriter.

I was almost thirteen at the time and he was an old man. I thought he was as old as any man could be, although he was probably well under sixty.

He said, "My boy, what is that contraption?"

I said, "It is a typewriter, sir."

"What is it for?" he said.

"It is for clear writing," I said, and handed him an example of typewriter print on paper.

"What is this writing on the paper?"

"Philosophical sayings."

"By which philosopher?" my great-uncle Garabed said.

"By myself," I said.

He sat on the bed, lighted a cigarette, then studied the sheet of paper and his great-nephew.

When he got up to go, he said, "Proceed, for it is not impossible to walk on water."

Even though he had said very little, there was no mistaking what he meant. Coming from him, a man famous for his fierce wit, this was approval, recognition and encouragement to keep on trying, and I felt much obliged to him.

EDITOR'S NOTE: *This recollection by William Saroyan, published March 2, 1947, was one of the first contributions to the "Words to Live By" series. A decade later we asked Mr. Saroyan if he had further words of wisdom to impart. In answer, he sent us the "sequel" which follows, another bit of philosophy from a different relative.*

Birth of an Author
II

BY

WILLIAM SAROYAN

"Have head examined."

—BAGRAT SAROYAN

TEN YEARS AGO in *This Week* I reported in an anecdote the words of my great-uncle Garabed Saroyan in 1921 when he visited my workroom, noticed my typewriter, asked what it was for, and was told by me, aged thirteen, that I meant to write philosophical sayings on it.

He said, "Proceed, for it is not impossible to walk on water."

Now it is another time, 1935; I am no longer thirteen, I am twenty-six. I have had one book published, writing is now my profession, and yet somehow I find that I need $100 in a hurry. Whom shall I turn to for this small loan? A member of the family, of course. From San Francisco I wired Bagrat Saroyan in Fresno for a loan of $100, half believing he would lend me $500. In less than two hours his reply came, collect: HAVE HEAD EXAMINED.

The telegram astonished, annoyed and delighted me, by turns. I put it in my pocket and walked to the public library. Every now and then on the way I brought it out and read it again, as if it were in Latin, or classical Armenian, and I hadn't quite got its meaning straight. At the public library I read around in a book for a couple of hours, but every now and then I just had to forget Tolstoi and read Bagrat again.

He wasn't half the writer Tolstoi was, but he was no slouch either.

I said to myself, "Well, take his advice. What else? After all, he's twenty years your senior and a Saroyan."

I knew no head examiner, so I decided to do the examining myself. I left the public library, walked around town, and then back home, examining all the while. The findings were enormous, varied, comic and holy. By the time I was back at my desk and typewriter I knew I didn't need $100 at all.

I began to write a new short story, aware that now at last I had everything—for that was what the process of examining had given me.

In the Saroyan family the phrase is now famous. It means all things to all men, and no nonsense either.

How to Grow

BY

LLOYD MORRIS

AUTHOR OF "POSTSCRIPT TO YESTERDAY"

"The only people who never make mistakes are those who never do anything."

—MY GRANDFATHER

SO MY grandfather told me, when I was a boy of ten. We were being taught wood carving at school. To surprise him on his birthday, I had undertaken to make a pair of bookends. Unfortunately, I botched the job. One was exactly like the model; the other was not. Holding them up before the class, the teacher ridiculed my handiwork. This humiliated me, but there was still worse to come. On the morning of Grandfather's sixty-fifth birthday I had to explain why I had no gift for him.

To me he seemed very old and very wise, and I dreaded

his censure, because he had scant patience with bunglers. He listened to me gravely, without comment. When I had finished, he spoke the words that I have quoted above. They comforted me then, as he intended, by restoring my damaged self-respect. Although I never forgot them, many years passed before I understood their real meaning.

Grandfather wanted me to realize that life itself provides for a margin of error. Day by day we have to decide and take action, often lacking the full knowledge that would assure our success. As a result, we can never completely avoid the possibility of a mistake. But to fear making a mistake is the worst mistake of all. Life constantly yields us second chances, and it is in grasping them that we put our previous failures to creative use. Since we learn by doing, we succeed only by having at *some* time failed.

Make a Weakness Pay Off

BY

DORE SCHARY

PLAYWRIGHT, MOTION PICTURE EXECUTIVE

"If you have a weakness make it work for you."
—MY MOTHER

MY MOTHER was a hard-working and very wise woman. Many years ago she observed to me, "If you have a weakness, make it work for you as a strength—and if you have a strength, don't abuse it into a weakness."

Through the years, and in the different jobs I have held, I have seen constant demonstrations of the truth of my mother's observations.

A person who chooses to call himself frank and candid can very easily find himself becoming tactless and cruel. A person who prides himself on being tactful can find eventually that he has become evasive and deceitful.

A person with firm convictions can become pigheaded. A person who is inclined to be temperate and judicious can sometimes turn into a man with weak convictions and banked fires of resolution.

Good habits of health too rigidly followed can make you a hypochondriac.

Hard work, unless balanced by relaxation of mind and body, may eventually destroy you.

Loyalty can lead to fanaticism. Caution can become timidity. Freedom can become license. Confidence can become arrogance. Humility can become servility.

All these are ways in which strength can become weakness. But the reverse is true too.

Destructiveness based on a desire to know what makes something tick can often be channeled into constructiveness directed at making it tick better.

Gullibility can be turned into understanding and compassion.

Restlessness can be turned into versatility.

Laziness can be turned into contemplation and study.

Extravagance can be turned into generosity.

I think of this often and, while I lead quite a regulated life, I very often deliberately break habits—change patterns

—merely to avoid the danger of extremes and open up new avenues of inner growth.

Look at that first line again: "If you have a weakness, make it work for you as a strength—and if you have a strength, don't abuse it into a weakness." Study it, apply it, and I think you will find comfort, strength and truth in it.

The Best Part of Life

BY

ANYA SETON

NOVELIST, AUTHOR OF "THE WINTHROP WOMAN"

"Stand still and look until you really see."
—MY FATHER

I WAS a restless little girl, greedy for sensations, hankering too much for the next moment, without savoring the now. My father, Ernest Thompson Seton, was a naturalist and a great admirer of our Indians. In both capacities he had learned the art of wonder—simple looking, without strain or self-consciousness, until he really *saw*.

Long ago, at our Connecticut home, he would take me on walks, which often bored me, for suddenly he would stop stock-still on the road, gazing up at a bank.

"What are you staring at, Daddy?" I would clamor. "*Do* let's go on!"

"Look, child!" he would answer, smiling. "What do you see?" And I would see nothing but a dull mass of stones and dead leaves, while I tugged at him impatiently. "Look again!' he would command, unmoving. And at last I learned to see what he did, the glimmering petals of spring beauties or hepatica, the turquoise glint of a fallen robin's egg, a baby rabbit peering out from under a toadstool, the chipped rosy quartz of an Indian arrowhead dropped three hundred years before.

Gradually I learned one of the most comforting truths in life—that the present moment is always filled with curious treasures, if we but quiet ourselves and look deep.

Too often through the years of marriage, motherhood and writing of my books, I have forgotten this lesson and plunged into hectic rush, until the mind and nerves get frazzled and the body therefore sickens. Then I'm stopped by the echo of my father's voice—"Wait a minute! What's the hurry? Stand still and look until you really see!"

Perhaps this command is easiest to follow with regard to nature and art, but it does not depend on these to yield its magic balm. There is no person, no situation which cannot cause wonder, if we will stop and gaze as though for the first time.

Goethe said, "The highest to which man can attain is wonder." And the faculty does seem to lead to humility and gratitude and happiness.

Young Philosophers Speaking

I

BY

PAUL GANDOLA

WHEN HE WAS SIX

"Every minute starts an hour."
—PAUL GANDOLA

EDITOR'S NOTE: Often the sayings on *This Week*'s "Words to Live By" page come from famous sources—the Bible or Shakespeare, or some book or legend handed down through the centuries. But not always. For anyone, anywhere, is capable of saying something that is worth remembering, and worth living by.

Take six-year-old Paul Gandola, of Rocky River, Ohio. He certainly wasn't trying to be a philosopher when he said the words reproduced above and sent us by his father. Rather, he was just looking at his father's watch, puzzling over the mystery of telling time. But the words he spoke stick in your mind. They are a reminder of the unfolding challenge and adventure that come just through being alive.

Every minute starts an hour. And every minute is a new opportunity. Each time the clock ticks you have a chance to start over, to say, do, think or feel something in such a way that you and the world are the better for it.

Young Philosophers Speaking

II

BY

FRANCESCA KERR

WHEN SHE WAS FOUR, AS RECALLED BY HER ACTRESS MOTHER, DEBORAH KERR

"I love you outside the line of numbers."
—FRANCESCA KERR

MY DAUGHTER Francesca was about four years old when she first became aware that numbers were not just new words in her vocabulary or names of digits, but that they can be useful to express quantity. This step, as all parents learn, follows the "so big" stage.

One memorable day, Francesca turned to me to express her love with the help of her new-found knowledge and said,

"Mummy, I love you ten times," followed by deep thought and "I love you twenty times."

After another short pause, she reached a breathless pinnacle with "I love you six hundred times."

A grateful hug and kiss from me produced a tiny frown and more concentrated thought which disappeared in a sigh of relief in her final outburst, "Mummy, I love you outside the line of the numbers."

My child's words touched me so deeply that I have never forgotten a moment of that scene, or the wisdom of her sudden discovery that you cannot measure love!

The insight that children "discover" never ceases to amaze me. Somehow their minds, uncluttered by the tensions of responsibility, can reach directly into the heart of a problem and make it brilliantly clear.

A knowledge that love is immeasurable is actually very subtle. And yet my four-year-old understood it completely, without the mechanics of logic—with only the instinct of the young. That day, that moment, my daughter knew what adults so often forget: we can neither demand nor give a love that can be counted or measured. We cannot measure love—and should not. But we can accept it, cherish it, nurture it, and thank the Lord for it.

PART SIX

Ways Of Life

A selection of tested rules for everyday living.

Grandfather's Quaker Dozen

BY

OLIVE IRELAND THEEN

Here are twelve rules, written long ago in a family Bible. They still fit today's problems.

WHEN I WAS a little girl, I often heard my grandfather tell about the stern, rigid rules his Quaker family lived by. They were called the "Quaker Dozen," and every good Quaker believed in and scrupulously followed them.

I thought my grandfather was very strict. His "living by the old school of thought" was difficult for me to understand. I couldn't find in it the freedom a child needs.

But later, when I read the rules again from the old family Bible, I realized there is less strictness—and more freedom—in this way of living than I have found in any other.

I have learned to carry the rules in my heart. I'm sure that if you carry them with you, you will find that the "Quaker Dozen" make good sense today—for all of us.

1. *Begin each day with a prayer*
2. *Work hard*
3. *Love your family*
4. *Make light of your troubles*
5. *Follow the Golden Rule*
6. *Read from the Bible*
7. *Show kindness*
8. *Read worthwhile books*
9. *Be clean and pure*
10. *Have charity in your heart*
11. *Be obedient and respectful*
12. *End the day in prayer*

For Very Young Philosophers Only

BY

WILL DURANT

PHILOSOPHER AND AUTHOR

Here are ten wise rules from a famous grandfather.

EDITOR'S NOTE: *Mr. Durant, as everyone knows, is the distinguished author of an impressive list of important books, including the multivolumed* The Story Of Civilization. *But when we asked him to contribute some thoughts to the "Words to Live By" page, he stepped out of his role as philosopher and historian into that of grandfather. The advice he gives here was written for his own three grandchildren.*

1. Begin the day with cleanliness. Keep your bathroom immaculate.

2. Before leaving your room in the morning put all discarded clothing into a dresser or a closet.

3. Dress yourself neatly; other people can judge us only by what they see, until they know us well; and their judgments will affect our progress and our happiness.

4. Enter into the life of the family and the community with good cheer; make little of your troubles, much of your good fortune.

5. Do not speak while another is speaking. Discuss, do not dispute. Absorb and acknowledge whatever truth you can find in opinions different from your own.

6. Be courteous and considerate to all, especially to those who oppose you.

7. Reduce to a minimum your reading, hearing, and watching of material intended for immature minds. The mind is formed by what it takes in. Don't be a wastebasket.

8. Do some studying every day; grow old while learning.

9. Combine external modesty with internal pride. Your modesty will make it easier for those around you to bear with you; your internal pride will stir you to shun meanness and sloth.

10. You will find in the Golden Rule the simplest and surest secret of happiness.

I Was Brought Up on These Words

BY

FIELD MARSHAL VISCOUNT MONTGOMERY

Two precepts from a famous general

"Fear God, Honor the Queen."

WHEN I WAS a young boy in Great Britain, Queen Victoria was our Queen and I was brought up on the above words. Now we have Queen Elizabeth II. I believe that now, as then, these words are the basis of character on which all else must be built. What follows explains why I think so.

"Fear God." This means that we must remember and practice the difference between right and wrong which has been taught us in our homes ever since we were old enough to crawl. A really decent man does not do the bad, mean

things which he knows are wrong. As his reward he enjoys a clear conscience and the love and respect of his fellow men.

"Honor the Queen." This, to an Englishman, is one phrase which sums up many values, but in one form or another they hold true all over the world. It calls upon us to be loyal and never to let down our country, our family or our friends. As we attain responsibility we learn to expect loyalty from those below us; we have no right to this unless we are loyal to those above us.

Next, it calls on us to be truthful. At times it takes courage to speak the truth. We must see to it that we can look a person straight in the face and tell him the truth.

Next, it calls on us to be honest and unselfish. We must learn that we gain far more satisfaction from doing something which benefits others than something which only benefits ourselves. We all learn as we grow older that we cannot expect always to take and never to give. Many of our fathers and forefathers gave their lives that we might live in the pleasant lands where our homes lie. We must see to it that we also are ready to give something of our life to the great destiny that lies ahead.

The phrase also reminds us that happiness will not be found purely in the search for enjoyment. True happiness is a frame of mind, and it comes from achievement through work. The greater the achievement, the more effort and hard work it needs—and the greater happiness it will give us.

Finally, it tells us to be adventurous. There are still great worlds to conquer—not through wars, but through learning in all the arts and sciences and above all through learning how to live in peace and comradeship with the peoples of all nations.

As a soldier, I like to sum things up. Here are the underlying ideas which seem to me important: *Remember what you have been taught about right and wrong, and stick to what is right when you are tempted to do what you know is wrong. Be truthful. Be honest. Be unselfish. Seek happiness through achievement, which results from hard work. Be adventurous in spirit. These are guideposts for all men and women of character.*

"Just for Today!"

BY

KENNETH L. HOLMES

DEAN OF MEN, LINFIELD COLLEGE,

MCMINNVILLE, OREGON

Nine resolutions to renew each morning.

SEVERAL YEARS AGO I had occasion to help a couple of my friends to make contact with Alcoholics Anonymous. In the process I was exposed to the teaching and philosophy of this movement. Though I am not eligible for membership myself, I have since carried in my billfold a little folder entitled *Just for Today,* which was issued by the local branch of Alcoholics Anonymous. I believe it holds a message for everybody, everywhere and every day. My copy is dog-eared and nearly worn out, but here is what these "Words to Live By" say:

Just for today, I will try to live through this day only, and not tackle my whole life problem at once. I can do something for twelve hours that would appall me if I felt that I had to keep it up for a lifetime.

Just for today, I will be happy. This assumes to be true what Abraham Lincoln said, that "most folks are as happy as they make up their minds to be."

Just for today, I will try to strengthen my mind. I will study. I will learn something useful. I will not be a mental loafer. I will read something that requires effort, thought and concentration.

Just for today, I will adjust myself to what is, and not try to adjust everything to my own desires. I will take my "luck" as it comes, and fit myself to it.

Just for today, I will exercise my soul in three ways: I will do somebody a good turn, and not get found out. I will do at least two things I don't want to do—just for exercise. I will not show anyone that my feelings are hurt; they may be hurt, but today I will not show it.

Just for today, I will be agreeable. I will look as well as I can, dress becomingly, talk low, act courteously, criticize not one bit, not find fault with anything and not try to improve or regulate anybody except myself.

Just for today, I will have a program. I may not follow it exactly, but I will have it. I will save myself from two pests: hurry and indecision.

Just for today, I will have a quiet half hour all by myself, and relax. During this half hour, sometime, I will try to get a better perspective of my life.

Just for today, I will be unafraid. Especially I will not be afraid to enjoy what is beautiful, and to believe that as I give to the world, so the world will give to me.

How to Stay Young

BY

BLANCHE McKEOWN

LIBRARIAN

"If a man does not make new acquaintances, as he advances through life, he will soon find himself left alone."

—DR. SAMUEL JOHNSON

I'M A LIBRARIAN in a large Southern city, and all day long I'm faced with elderly people who are sometimes confused, unhappy and resentful over their situation.

All this has started me thinking. I'm not old yet, but I'm not exactly in my first youth either, and I've begun wondering what I'll be like in a few years. It seems to me the key to the problem is boredom. Many older people are bored because they are lonely and idle, left to think too much about themselves.

What's the best cure for boredom? I found the answer in the quotation above. It's to forget yourself through activities which bring you in touch with people and ideas outside yourself.

And so, as my own special insurance against boredom, I've devised this four-point program, and I can testify that it really pays in terms of everyday happiness:

1. Join a church and become actively interested in some phase of its work.

2. Select one charitable activity and really work with it. Giving money is fine, of course, and good for the soul, but just as important is direct personal work which brings with it many new friends and associations.

3. Interest some young person in your line of work, and teach him to love it as you do.

4. Select some hobby that promises to be increasingly rewarding as you grow older.

With the help of these activities, I hope that I shall be able to go on building a state of mind which will make old age a pleasant, relaxed, contented period instead of a time of frustration. When the day comes for me to step aside to make room for the younger generation, I want to do it gracefully, without regrets or jealousy. I intend to keep on having a future instead of merely a past.

When You Can't Sleep

BY

A. P. HERBERT

BRITISH HUMORIST AND FORMER MEMBER OF PARLIAMENT

IT IS FOUR O'CLOCK in the morning—the worst hour of the day. You are awake, and worrying. You bear the burdens of the world. How are you to pay the income tax, find a house, get a better job, impress that pernickety boss? Your son's health, your daughter's behavior, the meals for tomorrow, the school bills—your poor head rambles round the troubles and the problems and scribbles incoherent lists of things you have to do. Will that wallpaper really be right? Is John good enough for Jane? And suppose there is a war? Poor, wandering head. You will never go to sleep again.

Yes, you will. You will say four simple things to yourself, many times. At each saying you will take a deep breath, and let it go. (Personally, at first, I open and close the eyes as well, in time with breathing, for if there is any light this helps to pull the mind out of that black whirling world of worry. But that is optional.)

You will say to yourself—and mean it:

"Fear Nothing."

Breathe, and let go. Open the eyes, see the light, and restfully close them. "Fear nothing." That takes care of the future. What a feeble soul you are to see so many phantoms! Then:

"Thank God."

That brings the past into the argument. How lucky, after all, you have been! What a good time, on the whole, you have had! And who said it was over? Next:

"Why Worry?"

Those words bring you face to face with yourself. Worry? A ridiculous state of mind! And what good does it do? So:

"All's Well."

Breathe very deep on that last triumphant chord—and start again. The bursting head is easier already; instead of plunging about in a murky jungle, it ambles comfortably on a straight white road—to the land of sleep. Go on. "Fear nothing. . . ." But think the magic words and believe them. Otherwise, you will be straying away to that wallpaper, that war again.

I have not just invented my sleepy sayings; I have used them for many years. They may not help you much if you are condemned to death, or suffering terrible pain—though, even then, who knows? But for the fretting four o'clocks of most of us they serve very well. Have yourself called at four tomorrow morning and try it.

How to Wake Up Smiling

BY

J. HARVEY HOWELLS

NOVELIST, PLAYWRIGHT, ADVERTISING MAN

"YOU FORGOT SOMETHING," said my six-year-old urgently as I bent to kiss him good night. He grabbed my hand. "You forgot to ask me what was the happiest thing that happened today."

"I'm sorry. So I did." I sat down on the edge of the bed.

At last came the whisper. "Catching that sand eel." A contented sigh. "My first fish." He snuggled into the pillow. " 'Night, Dad."

When it started I do not know. Nor do I know how, but this prayerlike ritual has been my own private blessing since beyond memory.

There is a moment of complete loneliness that comes to everyone every day. When the last good night has been mur-

mured and the head is on the pillow, the soul is utterly alone with its thoughts.

It is then that I ask myself, "What was the happiest thing that happened today?"

The waking hours may have been filled with stress and even distress; I have been in a highly competitive business all my life. But no matter what kind of day it has been, there is always a "happiest" thing.

Funnily enough, it's rarely a big thing. Mostly it's a fleeting loveliness. Waking to the honk of Canada geese on a crisp fall morning. An unexpected letter from a friend who doesn't write often. A cool swim on a broiling day. Listening to "Seventy-six Trombones." Camellias in the snow in an amazed New Orleans. My wife's face when she makes me laugh.

There's always something, and as a result I have never had a sleeping pill in my life. I doubt if my son will ever need one either—if he, too, remembers that happiness is not a goal dependent on some future event. It is with us every day if we make the conscious effort to recognize it.

PART SEVEN

My Own Words To Live By

"Make your own Bible. Select and collect all the words and sentences that in all your reading have been to you like the blast of triumph out of Shakespeare, Seneca, Moses, John and Paul."

—RALPH WALDO EMERSON

THE TOP TEN BY Daniel Starch
MY OWN WORDS chosen by the Reader

The Top Ten

BY

DANIEL STARCH

BUSINESS RESEARCH CONSULTANT

HERE IS a public-opinion survey which may be of special interest to readers of this book.

As an individual, I have long been a collector of "Words to Live By." As a statistician, I was anxious to know which sayings are most highly valued by Americans as a whole. So I worked out a "Words to Live By" survey. It began with a list of nearly one hundred famous sayings. This was then submitted to a sufficient number of selected persons throughout the country to give a cross-section opinion.

Here are the results of the poll, in order of preference, with the actual number of votes shown on the right. The sources given below are the earliest or the most widely known:

1. Do unto others as you would that they should do unto you. 1,237

2.	Know thyself.	1,125
3.	Anything that is worth doing at all is worth doing well.	744
4.	If at first you don't succeed, try, try again.	719
5.	The great essentials of happiness are something to do, something to love, and something to hope for.	697
6.	The only way to have a friend is to be one.	637
7.	As a man thinketh in his heart, so is he.	615
8.	Knowledge is power.	615
9.	Actions speak louder than words.	579
10.	An ounce of prevention is worth a pound of cure.	564

SOURCES: 1. Bible (paraphrase of Matthew and Luke). 2. Attributed originally by Plato to Socrates; also to the Delphic Oracle. 3. Earl of Chesterfield. 4. William E. Hickson 5. Unknown. 6. Ralph Waldo Emerson. 7. Bible (Proverbs). 8. Thomas Hobbes. 9. An ancient proverb, source unknown. 10. An old English proverb.

My Own Words to Live By

BY

THE READER

Index of Quotations

Index of Contributors

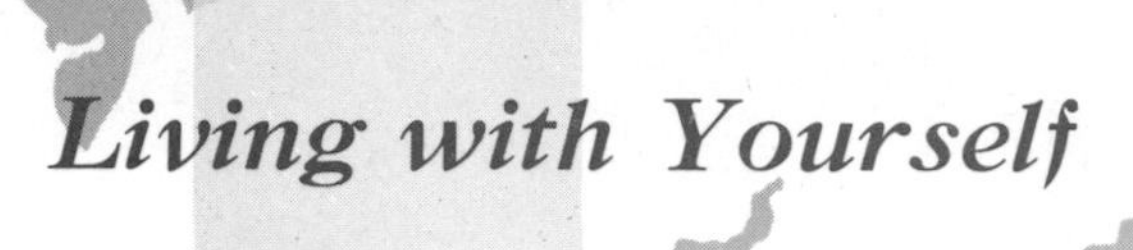

Living with Yourself

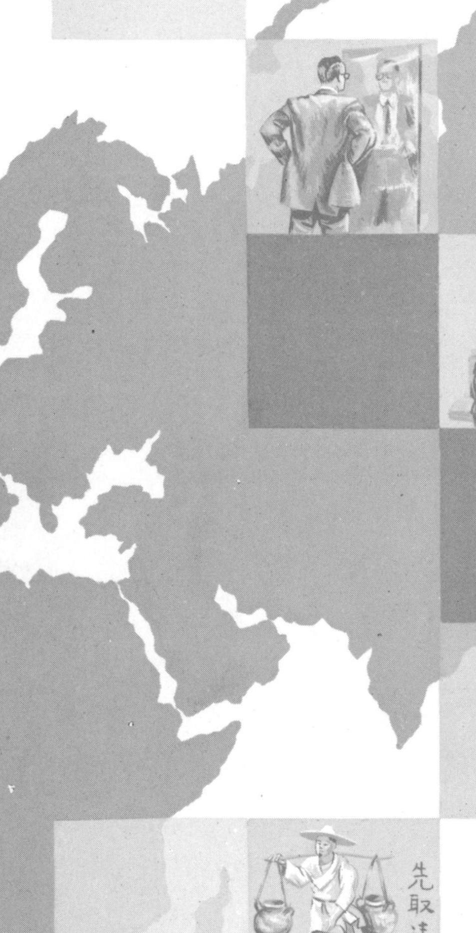

Living with other People